LINUX KERNEL

IN A NUTSHELL

Other Linux resources from O'Reilly

Related titles
Building Embedded Linux
   Systems
Linux Device Drivers
Linux in a Nutshell
Linux Pocket Guide

Running Linux
Understanding Linux
   Network Internals
Understanding the Linux
   Kernel

**Linux Books
Resource Center**
linux.oreilly.com is a complete catalog of O'Reilly's books on Linux and Unix and related technologies, including sample chapters and code examples.

Conferences
O'Reilly brings diverse innovators together to nurture the ideas that spark revolutionary industries. We specialize in documenting the latest tools and systems, translating the innovator's knowledge into useful skills for those in the trenches. Visit conferences.oreilly.com for our upcoming events.

**O'REILLY NETWORK
Safari
Bookshelf.**
Safari Bookshelf (*safari.oreilly.com*) is the premier online reference library for programmers and IT professionals. Conduct searches across more than 1,000 books. Subscribers can zero in on answers to time-critical questions in a matter of seconds. Read the books on your Bookshelf from cover to cover or simply flip to the page you need. Try it today for free.

LINUX
KERNEL

IN A NUTSHELL

Greg Kroah-Hartman

O'REILLY®

Beijing • Cambridge • Farnham • Köln • Paris • Sebastopol • Taipei • Tokyo

Linux Kernel in a Nutshell

by Greg Kroah-Hartman

Published by O'Reilly Media, Inc., 1005 Gravenstein Highway North, Sebastopol, CA 95472.

O'Reilly books may be purchased for educational, business, or sales promotional use. Online editions are also available for most titles (*safari.oreilly.com*). For more information, contact our corporate/institutional sales department: (800) 998-9938 or *corporate@oreilly.com*.

Editor: Andy Oram
Production Editor: Adam Witwer
Copyeditor: Mary Anne Weeks Mayo
Proofreader: Adam Witwer

Indexer: Ellen Troutman
Cover Designer: Karen Montgomery
Interior Designer: David Futato
Illustrators: Robert Romano and Jessamyn Read

Printing History:

December 2006:   First Edition.

RepKover. This book uses RepKover™, a durable and flexible lay-flat binding.

ISBN-10: 0-596-10079-5
ISBN-13: 978-0-596-10079-7
[M]

Table of Contents

Part IV. Additional Information

Preface

When the topic of this book was first presented to me, I dismissed it as something that was already covered by the plentiful documentation about the Linux kernel. Surely someone had already written down all of the basics needed in order to build, install, and customize the Linux kernel, because it seemed to be a very simple task to me.*

After digging through the different HOWTOs and the Linux kernel *Documentation* directory, I came to the conclusion that there was no one place where all of this information could be found. It could be gleaned by referencing a few files here, and a few outdated web sites there, but this was not acceptable for anyone who did not know exactly what they were looking for in the first place.

So this book was created with the goal of consolidating all of the existing information already scattered around the Internet about building the Linux kernel, as well as adding a lot of new and useful information that was not written down anywhere but had been learned by trial and error over my years of doing kernel development.

My secret goal of this book is to bring more people into the Linux kernel development fold. The act of building a customized kernel for your machine is one of the basic tasks needed to become a Linux kernel developer. The more people that try this out, and realize that there is not any real magic behind the whole Linux kernel process, the more people will be willing to jump in and help out in making the kernel the best that it can be.

---

* Disclaimer: I'm a Linux kernel developer by trade, so things that seem basic and simple to me at times are completely incomprehensible by most people, as my family continues to remind me.

Who This Book Is For

This book is intended to cover everything that is needed to know in order to properly build, customize, and install the Linux kernel. No programming experience is needed to understand and use this book.

Some familiarity with how to use Linux, and some basic command-line usage is expected of the reader.

This book is not intended to go into the programming aspects of the Linux kernel; there are many other good books listed in the Bibliography that already cover this topic.

How the Book Is Organized

This book is organized into four parts.

Part I, *Building the Kernel*, includes Chapters 1 through 6, which cover everything you need to know about retrieving, building, installing, and upgrading the Linux kernel, in more or less step-by-step fashion.

Chapter 1, *Introduction*
> This chapter explains when and why you would want to build the kernel.

Chapter 2, *Requirements for Building and Using the Kernel*
> This chapter covers the different programs and tools that are needed in order to properly build the kernel. It also covers a number of different programs that are tied very closely to the kernel, how to determine the needed version of the programs, and where to find them.

Chapter 3, *Retrieving the Kernel Source*
> This chapter discusses how the different Linux kernel versions relate to each other, where to retrieve the Linux kernel source code, and how to download it properly.

Chapter 4, *Configuring and Building*
> This chapter explains how to configure and properly build the Linux kernel.

Chapter 5, *Installing and Booting from a Kernel*
> This chapter shows how to install the kernel that has been built properly, and then boot into that kernel version.

Chapter 6, *Upgrading a Kernel*
> This chapter explains how to upgrade a kernel that was previously built to a newer version without having to start over from nothing.

Part II, *Major Customizations*, consists of Chapters 7 and 8, which describe how to properly configure the kernel based on the hardware present in the system, and provides a number of different "recipes" for common configurations.

Chapter 7, *Customizing a Kernel*
> This chapter discusses how to customize the kernel for the hardware that is present on the system. It goes over a variety of different ways to determine

what options should be selected and provides some simple scripts to help with the task.

Chapter 8, *Kernel Configuration Recipes*
This chapter explains how to configure the kernel for a variety of common situations.

Part III, *Kernel Reference*, consists of Chapters 9 through 11. These chapters provide a reference to the different kernel command line options, the kernel build options, and a select few of the different kernel configuration options.

Chapter 9, *Kernel Boot Command-Line Parameter Reference*
This chapter details all of the different command-line options that can be passed to the kernel, and what the different options do.

Chapter 10, *Kernel Build Command-Line Reference*
This chapter describes the different command line options that are available when building the kernel and how to use them.

Chapter 11, *Kernel Configuration Option Reference*
This chapter focuses on a few of the more popular and important Linux kernel configuration options.

Part IV, *Additional Information*

Appendix A, *Helpful Utilities*
This chapter introduces a number of very good and handy tools that everyone who wishes to track the latest Linux kernel version should use.

Appendix B, *Bibliography*
This chapter offers a list of useful references that you can use to track down more information on building your Linux kernel.

Online Version and License

This book is freely available under the Creative Commons "Attribution-ShareAlike" license, Version 2.5. This license can be seen in its entirety at *http://creativecommons.org/licenses/by-sa/2.5/*. The full book is also available online at *http://www.kroah.com/lkn*.

Conventions Used in This Book

This book uses the following typographical conventions:

Italic
Indicates progams, tools, commands and command options, distribution packages, files, directories, usernames, and hostnames. Also indicates nomenclature that we've not previously used and emphasized words.

Constant Width
Indicates strings used for kernel configuration, as well as a few special terms such as device names. Also used to show command output and the contents of text and program files.

Constant Width Bold

Used in examples to indicate commands or other text that should be typed literally by the user.

Constant Width Italic

Indicates text that you should replace with your own values; for example, your own name or password. When this appears as part of text that you should type in, it is shown as ***Constant Width Italic Bold***.

`#, $`

Used in some examples as the root shell prompt (#) and as the user prompt ($) under the Bourne or bash shell.

Indicates a tip, suggestion, or general note.

Indicates a warning or caution.

Using Shell Scripts

This book is here to help you get your job done. In general, you may use the shell scripts in this book in your own scripts and documentation. You do not need to contact us for permission. The major scripts can be downloaded from the book's web site on O'Reilly Media, *http://www.oreilly.com/catalog/9780596100797*.

We appreciate, but do not require, attribution. An attribution usually includes the title, author, publisher, and ISBN. For example: "*Linux Kernel in a Nutshell* by Greg Kroah-Hartman. Copyright 2007 O'Reilly Media, Inc., 978-0-596-10079-7."

If you feel your use of code examples falls outside fair use or the permission given above, feel free to contact us at *permissions@oreilly.com*.

Safari® Enabled

When you see a Safari® enabled icon on the cover of your favorite technology book, that means the book is available online through the O'Reilly Network Safari Bookshelf.

Safari offers a solution that's better than e-books. It's a virtual library that lets you easily search thousands of top tech books, cut and paste code samples, download chapters, and find quick answers when you need the most accurate, current information. Try it free at *http://safari.oreilly.com*.

How to Contact Us

We have tested and verified all of the information in this book to the best of our ability, but you may find that features have changed (or even that we have made mistakes!). Please let us know about any errors you find, as well as your suggestions for future editions, by writing:

O'Reilly Media, Inc.
1005 Gravenstein Highway North
Sebastopol, CA 95472
800-998-9938 (in the United States or Canada)
707-829-0515 (international/local)
707-829-0104 (fax)

You can also send us messages electronically. To be put on the mailing list or request a catalog, send email to:

info@oreilly.com

To ask technical questions or comment on the book, send email to:

bookquestions@oreilly.com

We have a web site for the book, where we'll list examples, errata, and any plans for future editions. You can access this page at:

http://www.oreilly.com/catalog/9780596100797

Acknowledgments

Thanks first go to my wonderful wife Shannon and my beautiful children Madeline and Griffin for their understanding and patience while I took the time to work on this book. Without their support and prodding, this book would have never been completed. Special thanks to Shannon for getting me into Linux kernel development in the first place. Without her effort, I would be still doing some odd embedded programming job, and would have never discovered this great community in which to work in.

My editor, Andy Oram, is the driving force behing this book, shaping it into something that is both readable and informative. His editing skills and patience as deadlines flew by were instrumental in the creation and completion of this book.

Also a big thanks go to the original editor of this book, David Brickner, for giving me the chance to work on this project and believing that I could complete it, despite the first version weighing in at over 1,000 pages.

The technical reviewers for this book were amazing, catching all of the numerous mistakes and pointing out omissions that needed to be filled. The reviewers were (in alphabetic order by first name), Christian Benvenuti, Christian Morgner, Golden G. Richard III, Jean Delvare, Jerry Cooperstein, Michael Boerner, Rik van Riel, and Robert Day. Any remaining problems are due to me, and not their excellent skills.

A special thanks to Randy Dunlap for going over the kernel boot parameters with a fine-tooth comb and pointing out issues in that chapter. Also to Kay Sievers, who helped immensely with all of the chapter on customizing the kernel, and who provided the script at the end of that same chapter. Without his sysfs help and knowledge, that chapter would not have been feasible.

And a final special thanks to my sixth grade English teacher, Ms. Gruber, for teaching me that writing was something that was possible to do, and showing me the enjoyment in doing it. Without that start, none of this would have been attainable.

Building the Kernel

This part of the book shows how to download, build, and install the kernel. It is largely a step-by-step guide.

Introduction

Despite its large code base (over seven million lines of code), the Linux kernel is the most flexible operating system that has ever been created. It can be tuned for a wide range of different systems, running on everything from a radio-controlled model helicoptor, to a cell phone, to the majority of the largest supercomputers in the world. By customizing the kernel for your specific environment, it is possible to create something that is both smaller and faster than the kernel provided by most Linux distributions. This book will go into how to build and install a custom kernel, and provide some hints on how to enable specific options that you will probably wish to use for different situations.

No Linux distribution provides the exact kernel most of its users want. Modern distributions have gotten very accommodating, compiling in support for every known device, for sound, and even for power conservation. But you will likely have a need that's different from the majority of users (and every distribution has to try to meet the needs of the majority). You may just have different hardware. And when a new kernel comes out, you may want to start using it without waiting for a distribution to be built around it.

For a host of reasons, you will want during your Linux career to sometimes build a kernel, or to tweak the parameters of one you are running. This book gives you the information you need to understand the kernel from a user's point of view, and to make the most common changes.

There are also good reasons to remove features from the kernel, particularly if you are running it on an embedded system or one with a small form factor.

When tweaking, it's helpful to understand the internals of kernel behavior. These are beyond the scope of this book, except for brief summaries that appear with certain options. Appendix B includes references to other books and material that can give you more background.

Using This Book

Do not configure or build your kernel with superuser permissions enabled!

This warning is the most important thing to remember while working through the steps in this book. Everything in this book—downloading the kernel source code, uncompressing it, configuring the kernel, and building it—should be done as a normal user on the machine. Only the two or three commands it takes to install a new kernel should be done as the superuser (*root*).

There have been bugs in the kernel build process in the past, causing some special files in the */dev* directory to be deleted if the user had superuser permissions while building the Linux kernel.* There are also issues that can easily arise when uncompressing the Linux kernel with superuser rights, as some of the files in the kernel source package will not end up with the proper permissions and will cause build errors later.

The kernel source code should also never be placed in the */usr/src/linux/* directory, as that is the location of the kernel that the system libraries were built against, not your new custom kernel. Do not do any kernel development under the */usr/src/* directory tree at all, but only in a local user directory where nothing bad can happen to the system.

---

* This took quite a while to fix, as none of the primary kernel developers build kernels as root, so they did not suffer from the bug. A number of weeks went by before it was finally determined that the act of building the kernel was the problem. A number of kernel developers half-jokingly suggested that the bug remain in, to help prevent anyone from building the kernel as root, but calmer heads prevailed and the bug in the build system was fixed.

2

Requirements for Building and Using the Kernel

This chapter describes the programs you need to configure a kernel, build it, and successfully boot it. It's a smart idea to consult the file *Documentation/Changes* to verify the specific version number you should have of each tool described in this chapter. This chapter was based on the 2.6.18 kernel, and describes the versions of tools that work with that kernel. If you are using a different kernel, please verify that you have the required versions as specified in this file, or things might not work properly and it can be very hard to determine what went wrong.

Tools to Build the Kernel

Most Linux distributions offer an installation option to install a range of kernel hacking packages. If your distribution offers this option, it is easiest to install this instead of trying to track down all of the individual programs that are needed for this task.

Only three packages that are needed in order to successfully build a kernel: a compiler, a linker, and a *make* utility. This section describes the contents of each package.

Compiler

The Linux kernel is written in the C programming language, with a small amount of assembly language in some places. To build the kernel, the gcc C compiler must be used. Most Linux distributions have a package entitiled *gcc* that should be installed. If you wish to download the compiler and build it yourself, you can find it at *http://gcc.gnu.org*.

As of the 2.6.18 kernel release, the 3.2 version of *gcc* is the oldest that can properly build a working kernel. Be warned that getting the most recent *gcc* version is not always a good idea. Some of the newest *gcc* releases don't build the kernel properly, so unless you wish to help debug compiler bugs, it is not recommended that you try them out.

To determine which version of *gcc* you have on your system, run the following command:

```
$ gcc --version
```

Linker

The C compiler, *gcc*, does not do all of the compiling on its own. It needs an additional set of tools known as *binutils* to do the linking and assembling of source files. The *binutils* package also contains useful utilities that can manipulate object files in lots of useful ways, such as to view the contents of a library.

binutils can usually be found in a distribution package called (not surprisingly) *binutils*. If you wish to download and install the package yourself, you can find it at *http://www.gnu.org/software/binutils*.

As of the 2.6.18 kernel release, the 2.12 release of *binutils* is the oldest that can successfully link the kernel. To determine which version of *binutils* you have on your system, run the following command:

```
$ ld -v
```

make

make is a tool that walks the kernel source tree to determine which files need to be compiled, and then calls the compiler and other build tools to do the work in building the kernel. The kernel requires the GNU version of *make*, which can usually be found in a package called *make* for your distribution.

If you wish to download and install *make* youself, you can find it at *http://www.gnu.org/software/make*.

As of the 2.6.18 kernel release, the 3.79.1 release of *make* is the oldest that can properly build the kernel. It is recommended that you install the latest stable version of *make*, because newer versions are known to work faster at processing the build files.

To determine which version of *make* you have on your system, run the following command:

```
$ make --version
```

Tools to Use the Kernel

While the version of the kernel that is running does not usually affect any user application, there are a small number of program for which the kernel version is important. This section describes a number of tools that are probably already installed on your Linux system. If you upgrade your kernel to a version different from the one that came with your distribution, some of these packages may also need to be upgraded in order for the system to work properly.

util-linux

The *util-linux* package is a collection of small utilities that do a wide range of different tasks. Most of these utilities handle the mounting and creation of disk partitions and manipulation of the hardware clock in the system.

If you wish to download and install the *util-linux* package yourself, you can find it at *http://www.kernel.org/pub/linux/utils/util-linux*.

As of the 2.6.18 kernel release, the 2.10 release of *util-linux* is the oldest that works properly. It is recommended that you install the latest version of this package, because new version support new features added to the kernel. Bind mounts are one example of an option in newer kernels, and a newer version of *util-linux* is needed in order to have them work properly.

To determine which version of the *util-linux* package you have on your system, run the following command:

```
$ fdformat --version
```

module-init-tools

The *module-init-tools* package is needed if you wish to use Linux kernel modules. A *kernel module* is a loadable chunk of code that can be added to or removed from the kernel while the kernel is running. It is useful to compile device drivers as modules and then load only the ones that correspond to the hardware present in the system. All Linux distributions use modules in order to load only the needed drivers and options for the system based on the hardware present, instead of being forced to build all possible drivers and options in the kernel in one large chunk. Modules save memory by loading just the code that is needed to control the machine properly.

The kernel module loading process underwent a radical change in the 2.6 kernel release. The linker for the module (the code that resolves all symbols and figures out how to put the pieces together in memory) is now built into the kernel, which makes the userspace tools quite small. Older distributions have a package called *modutils* that does not work properly with the 2.6 kernel. The *module-init-tools* package is what you need to get the 2.6 kernel to work properly with modules.

If you wish to download and install the *module-init-tools* package yourself, you can find it at *http://www.kernel.org/pub/linux/utils/kernel/module-init-tools*.

As of the 2.6.18 kernel release, the 0.9.10 release of *module-init-tools* is the oldest version that works properly. It is recommended that the latest version of this package be installed, as new features added to the kernel can be used by newer versions of this package. Blacklisting modules to prevent them from being automatically loaded by the *udev* package is one such option that is present in newer versions of *module-init-tools*, but not older ones.

To determine which version of the *module-init-tools* package you have on your system, run the following command:

```
$ depmod -V
```

Filesystem-Specific Tools

A wide range of tools specific to particular filesystems are necessary to create, format, configure, and fix disk partitions. The *util-linux* package has a few of these utilities, but some of the more popular filesystems have separate packages that contain the necessary programs.

ext2/ext3/ext4

The *ext3* and experimental *ext4* filesystems are upgrades of *ext2* and can be managed with the same tools; any recent version of an *ext2*-based tool can work with the other two filesystems as well.

To work with any of these filesystems, you must have the *e2fsprogs* package. If you wish to download and install this package yourself, you can find it at *http://e2fsprogs.sourceforge.net*.

As of the 2.6.18 kernel release, the 1.29 release of *e2fsprogs* is the oldest that works properly with the kernel. It is highly recommended that you use the newest version in order to take advantage of newer features in the *ext3* and *ext4* filesystems.

To determine which version of *e2fsprogs* you have on your system, run the following command:

```
$ tune2fs
```

JFS

To use the JFS filesystem from IBM, you must have the *jfsutils* pacakge. If you wish to download and install this package yourself, you can find it at *http://jfs.sourceforge.net*.

As of the 2.6.18 kernel release, the 1.1.3 release of *jfsutils* is the oldest that works properly with the kernel. To determine which version of *jfsutils* you have on your system, run the following command:

```
$ fsck.jfs -V
```

ReiserFS

To use the ReiserFS filesystem, you must have the *reiserfsprogs* package. If you wish to download and install this package yourself, you can find it at *http://www.namesys.com/download.html*.

As of the 2.6.18 kernel release, the 3.6.3 release of *reiserfsprogs* is the oldest that works properly with the kernel. To determine which version of *reiserfsprogs* you have on your system, run the following command:

```
$ reiserfsck -V
```

XFS

To use the XFS filesystem from SGI, you must have the *xfsprogs* package. If you wish to download and install this package yourself, you can find it at *http://oss.sgi.com/projects/xfs*.

As of the 2.6.18 kernel release, the 2.6.0 release of *xfsprogs* is the oldest that works properly with the kernel. To determine which version of *xfsprogs* you have on your system, run the following command:

```
$ xfs_db -V
```

Quotas

To use the quota functionality of the kernel, you must have the *quota-tools* package.* This package includes programs that let you set quotas on users, provide statistics on the amount of quota being used by different users, and issue warnings when people get too close to using up their available filesystem quota.

If you wish to download and install this package yourself, you can find it at *http://sourceforge.net/projects/linuxquota*.

As of the 2.6.18 kernel release, the 3.09 release of *quota-tools* is the oldest that works properly with the kernel. To determine which version of *quota-tools* you have on your system, run the following command:

```
$ quota -V
```

NFS

To use the NFS filesystem properly, you must have the *nfs-utils* package.† This package includes programs that let you mount NFS partitions as a client, and run an NFS server.

If you wish to download and install this package yourself, you can find it at *http://nfs.sf.net*.

As of the 2.6.18 kernel release, the 1.0.5 release of *nfs-utils* is the oldest that works properly with the kernel To determine which version of *nfs-utils* you have on your system, run the following command:

```
$ showmount --version
```

Other Tools

There are a few other important programs that are closely tied to the kernel version. These programs are not usually required in order for the kernel to work properly, but they enable access to different types of hardware and functions.

---

* Some distributions, notably Debian, call this package *quota* instead of *quota-tools*.

† Some distributions, notably Debian, call this package *nfs-common* instead of *nfs-utils*.

udev

udev is a program that enables Linux to provide a persistent device-naming system in the */dev* directory. It also provides a dynamic */dev*, much like the one provided by the older (and now removed) *devfs* filesystem. Almost all Linux distributions use *udev* to manage the */dev* directory, so it is required in order to properly boot the machine.

Unfortunately, *udev* relies on the structure of */sys*, which has been known to change from time to time with kernel releases. Some of these changes in the past have been known to break *udev*, so that your machine will not boot properly. If you have the latest version of *udev* recommended for your kernel and have problems with it working properly, please contact the *udev* developers on the mailing list available at *linux-hotplug-devel@lists.sourceforge.net*.

It is highly recommended that you use the version of *udev* that comes with your Linux distribution, as it is tied into the distribution specific boot process very tightly. But if you wish to upgrade *udev* on your own, you can find it at *http:// www.kernel.org/pub/linux/utils/kernel/hotplug/udev.html*.

As of the 2.6.18 kernel release, the 081 release of *udev* is the oldest that works properly with the kernel. It is recommended that you use the latest version of *udev*, because it will work better with newer kernels, due to changes in how *udev* and the kernel communicate.

To determine which version of *udev* you have on your system, run the following command:

```
$ udevinfo -V
```

Process tools

The package *procps* includes the commonly used tools *ps* and *top*, as well as many other handy tools for managing and monitoring processes running on the system.

If you wish to download and install this package yourself, you can find it at *http:// procps.sourceforge.net*.

As of the 2.6.18 kernel release, the 3.2.0 release of *procps* is the oldest that works properly with the kernel. To determine which version of *procps* you have on your system, run the following command:

```
$ ps --version
```

PCMCIA tools

In order to properly use PCMCIA devices with Linux, a userspace helper program must be used to set up the devices. For older kernel versions, this program was called *pcmcia-cs*, but that has been replaced with a much simpler system called *pcmciautils*. If you wish to use PCMCIA devices, you must have this package installed for them to work properly.

If you wish to download and install this package yourself, you can find it at *ftp://ftp.kernel.org/pub/linux/utils/kernel/pcmcia.*

As of the 2.6.18 kernel release, the 004 release of *pcmciautils* is the oldest that works properly with the kernel. But the latest version is recommended in order to take advantage of newer features in the PCMCIA subsystem, such as automatic driver loading when new devices are found.

To determine which version of *pcmciautils* you have on your system, run the following command:

```
$ pccardctl -V
```

Requirements

3

Retrieving the Kernel Source

When you're building your own kernel, you want the latest stable release. Many distributions provide their own packages of kernel sources, but these are rarely the most cutting-edge, recent versions. The distribution packages have the advantage of being built to be compatible with the compiler and other tools provided by the distribution (Chapter 2 explains the importance of their being compatible) but they may not end up providing the functionality or performance you want. If you can create your own environment with the latest kernel, compiler, and other tools, you will be able to build exactly what you want. This chapter focuses on determining which kernel sources to download, and how to obtain them.

What Tree to Use

In the past, the Linux kernel was split into only two trees, the "development" branch and the "stable" branch. The *development branch* was denoted by an odd number for the second release number, while the *stable branch* used even numbers. So, as an example, the 2.5.25 release was a development kernel, while the 2.4.25 release is a stable release.

But after the 2.6 series was created, the kernel developers decided to abandon this method of having two separate trees, and declared that all 2.6 kernel releases would be considered "stable," no matter how quickly development was happening. The few months between the major 2.6 releases would allow kernel developers the time to add new features and then stabilize them in time for the next release. Combined with this, a "-stable" kernel branch has been created that releases bug fixes and security updates for the past kernel release, before the next major 2.6 release happens.

This is all best explained with some examples, illustrated in Figure 3-1. The kernel team released the 2.6.17 kernel as a stable release. Then the developers started working on new features and started releasing the *-rc* versions as development kernels so that people could help test and debug the changes. After everyone agreed that the development release was stable enough, it was released as the 2.6.18 kernel. This whole cycle usually takes about two to three months, depending on a variety of factors.

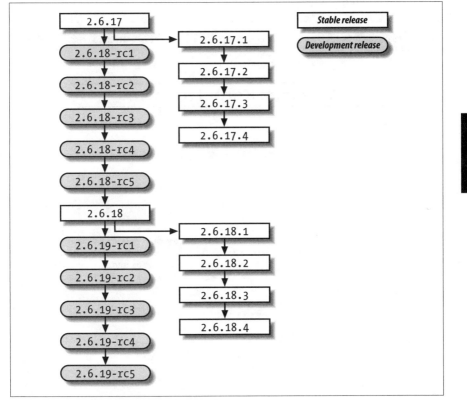

Figure 3-1. Kernel development release cycle

While the development of the new features was happening, the 2.6.17.1, 2.6.17.2, and other stable kernel versions were released, containing bug fixes and security updates.

If you wish to just use the latest kernel for your work, it is recommended that you use the stable kernel releases. If you wish to help the kernel developers test the features of the next kernel release and give them feedback, use the development kernel release. For the purpose of this chapter, we will assume that you are using a stable kernel release.

Where to Find the Kernel Source

All of the source code for the Linux kernel can be found on one of the *kernel.org* sites, a worldwide network of servers that mirror the Linux source code, enabling anyone to find a local server close to him. This allows the main kernel servers to be responsive to the mirror sites, and lets users download the needed files as quickly as possible.

The main *http://www.kernel.org* site shows all of the current kernel versions for the various different kernel trees, as shown in Figure 3-2.

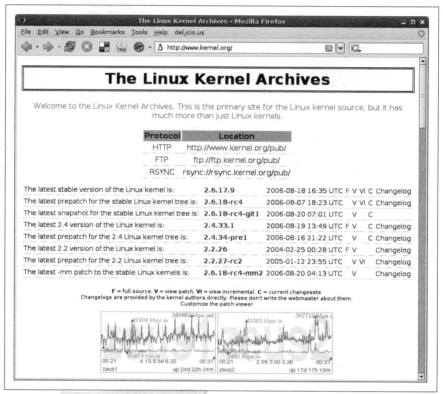

Figure 3-2. The main kernel.org web site

To download the latest stable kernel version, click on the *F* character on the line for the kernel version. This will download the full source tree. Or you can navigate to the proper subdirectory for all of the 2.6 kernel versions, *http://www.us.kernel.org/pub/linux/kernel/v2.6/*, shown in Figure 3-3.

It is also possible to download the kernel source from the command line, using the *wget* or *curl* utilities, both of which should come with your Linux distribution.

To download the 2.6.17.8 kernel version using *wget*, enter:

```
$ wget http://www.kernel.org/pub/linux/kernel/v2.6/linux-2.6.17.8.tar.gz
--17:44:55--  http://www.kernel.org/pub/linux/kernel/v2.6/linux-2.6.17.8.
tar.gz
           => `linux-2.6.17.8.tar.gz'
Resolving www.kernel.org... 204.152.191.5, 204.152.191.37
Connecting to www.kernel.org|204.152.191.5|:80... connected.
HTTP request sent, awaiting response... 200 OK
```

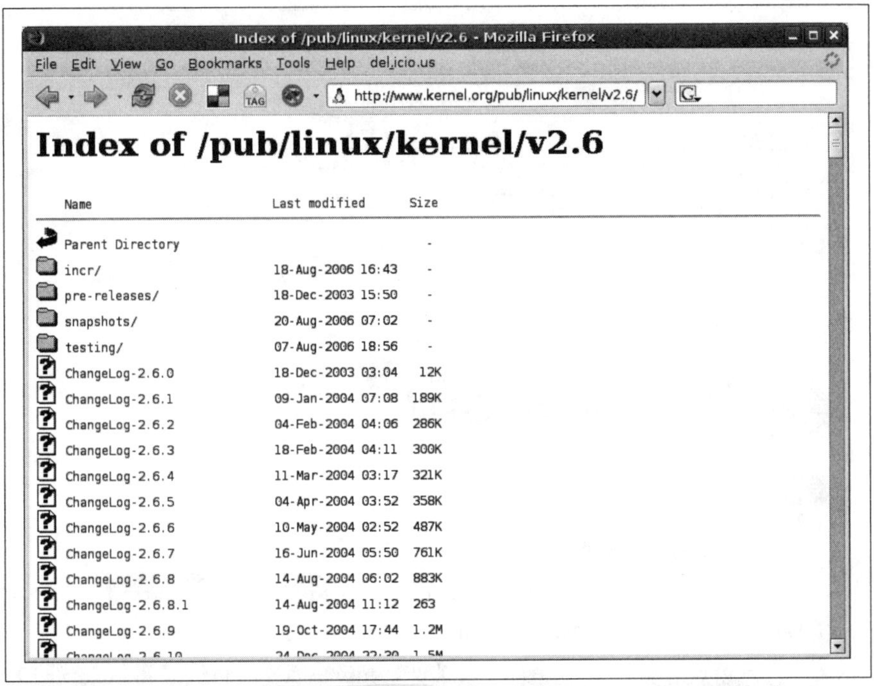

Figure 3-3. The 2.6 kernel source directory

```
Length: 51,707,742 (49M) [application/x-gzip]
100%[=============================================>] 51,707,742    35.25K/s
ETA 00:00
18:02:48 (47.12 KB/s) - `linux-2.6.17.8.tar.gz' saved [51707742/51707742]
```

To download it using *curl*:

```
$ curl http://www.kernel.org/pub/linux/kernel/v2.6/linux-2.6.17.8.tar.gz \
-o linux-2.6.17.8.tar.gz
  % Total    % Received % Xferd  Average Speed   Time    Time     Time
Current
                                 Dload  Upload   Total   Spent    Left
Speed
100 49.3M  100 49.3M    0     0  50298      0  0:17:08  0:17:08 --:--:--
100k
```

For a quick and easy way to determine the latest kernel versions, use the information available at *http://www.kernel.org/kdist/finger_banner*, illustrated by Figure 3-4.

What to Do with the Source

Now that you have downloaded the proper kernel source, where is it supposed to go? We suggest creating a local directory in your home directory called *linux* to hold all of the different kernel source files:

```
$ mkdir ~/linux
```

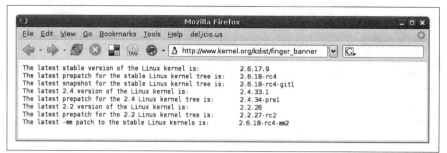

Figure 3-4. Latest kernel version

Now move the source code into this directory:

```
$ mv ~/linux-2.6.17.8.tar.gz ~/linux/
```

And go into the *linux* directory:

```
$ cd ~/linux
$ ls
linux-2.6.17.8.tar.gz
```

Now that the source code is in the proper directory, uncompress the tree:

```
$ tar -xzvf linux-2.6.17.8.tar.gz
```

The screen will be filled with files that are uncompressed, and you will be left with the following in the *linux/* directory:

```
$ ls
linux-2.6.17.8.tar.gz
linux-2.6.17.8/
```

4

Configuring and Building

Now that you have downloaded the source for your selected kernel version and installed it into a local directory, it is time to build the code. The first step is to configure the kernel with the appropriate options; the kernel can then be compiled. Both tasks are done through the standard *make* utility.

Creating a Configuration

The kernel configuration is kept in a file called *.config* in the top directory of the kernel source tree. If you have just expanded the kernel source code, there will be no *.config* file, so it needs to be created. It can be created from scratch, created by basing it on the "default configuration," taken from a running kernel version, or taken from a distribution kernel release. We will cover the first two methods here, and the last two methods in Chapter 7.

Configuring from Scratch

The most basic method of configuring a kernel is to use the *make config* method:

```
$ cd linux-2.6.17.10
$ make config
  make config
scripts/kconfig/conf arch/i386/Kconfig
*
* Linux Kernel Configuration
*
*
* Code maturity level options
*
Prompt for development and/or incomplete code/drivers (EXPERIMENTAL) [Y/n/?]
Y
*
* General setup
*
```

```
Local version - append to kernel release (LOCALVERSION) []
Automatically append version information to the version string
(LOCALVERSION_AUTO) [Y/n/?] Y
...
```

The kernel configuration program will step through every configuration option and ask you if you wish to enable this option or not. Typically, your choices for each option are shown in the format [Y/m/n/?] The capitalized letter is the default, and can be selected by just pressing the Enter key. The four choices are:

y   Build directly into the kernel.

n   Leave entirely out of the kernel.

m   Build as a module, to be loaded if needed.

?   Print a brief descriptive message and repeat the prompt.

The kernel contains almost two thousand different configuration options, so being asked for every individual one will take a very long time. Luckily, there is an easier way to configure a kernel: base the configuration on a pre-built configuration.

Default Configuration Options

Every kernel version comes with a "default" kernel configuration. This configuration is loosely based on the defaults that the kernel maintainer of that architecture feels are the best options to be used. In some cases, it is merely the configuration that is used by the kernel maintainer himself for his personal machines. This is true for the i386 architecture, where the default kernel configuration matches closely what Linus Torvalds uses for his main development machine.

To create this default configuration, do the following:

```
$ cd linux-2.6.17.10
$ make defconfig
```

A huge number of configuration options will scroll quickly by the screen, and a *.config* file will be written out and placed in the kernel directory. The kernel is now successfully configured, but it should be customized to your machine in order to make sure it will operate correctly.

Modifying the Configuration

Now that we have a basic configuration file created, it should be modified to support the hardware you have present in the system. For details on how to find out which configuration options you need to select to achieve this, please see Chapter 7. Here we will show you how to select the options you wish to change.

There are three different interactive kernel configuration tools: a terminal-based one called *menuconfig*, a GTK+-based graphical one called *gconfig*, and a QT-based graphical one called *xconfig*.

Console Configuration Method

The *menuconfig* way of configuring a kernel is a console-based program that offers a way to move around the kernel configuration using the arrow keys on the keyboard. To start up this configuration mode, enter:

```
$ make menuconfig
```

You will be shown a screen much like Figure 4-1.

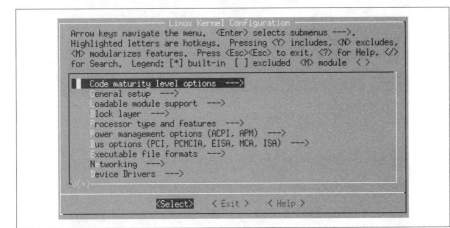

Figure 4-1. Initial menuconfig screen

The instructions for navigating through the program, and the meanings of the different characters, are shown at the top of the screen. The rest of the screen containing the different kernel configuration options.

The kernel configuration is divided up into sections. Each section contains options that correspond to a specific topic. Within those sections can be sub-sections for various specialized topics. As an example, all kernel device drivers can be found under the main menu option Device Drivers. To enter that menu, move the arrow key down nine times until the line Device Drivers ---> is highlighted, as shown in Figure 4-2.

Then press the Enter key. It will move you into the Device Drivers submenu and show it as illustrated in Figure 4-3.

You can continue to move down through the menu hierarchy the same way. To see the Generic Driver Options submenu, press Enter again, and you will see the three options shown in Figure 4-4.

The first two options have a [*] mark by them. That means that this option is selected (by virtue of the * being in the middle of the [ ] characters), and that this option is a yes-or-no option. The third option has a < > marking, showing that this option can be built into the kernel (Y), built as a module (M), or left out altogether (N).

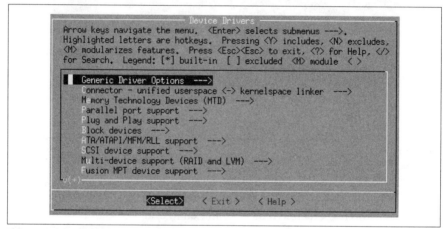

```
┌───────────────────── Linux Kernel Configuration ─────────────────────┐
│ Arrow keys navigate the menu.  <Enter> selects submenus --->.         │
│ Highlighted letters are hotkeys.  Pressing <Y> includes, <N> excludes,│
│ <M> modularizes features.  Press <Esc><Esc> to exit, <?> for Help, </>│
│ for Search.  Legend: [*] built-in  [ ] excluded  <M> module  < >      │
│ ┌───────────────────────────────────────────────────────────────────┐ │
│ │    General setup  --->                                            │ │
│ │    Loadable module support  --->                                 │ │
│ │    Block layer  --->                                             │ │
│ │    Processor type and features  --->                             │ │
│ │    Power management options (ACPI, APM)  --->                    │ │
│ │    Bus options (PCI, PCMCIA, EISA, MCA, ISA)  --->               │ │
│ │    Executable file formats  --->                                 │ │
│ │    Networking  --->                                              │ │
│ │    Device Drivers  --->                                          │ │
│ │    File systems  --->                                            │ │
│ └───────────────────────────────────────────────────────────────────┘ │
│              <Select>    < Exit >    < Help >                         │
└───────────────────────────────────────────────────────────────────────┘
```

Figure 4-2. Device Drivers option selected

```
┌──────────────────────────── Device Drivers ──────────────────────────┐
│ Arrow keys navigate the menu.  <Enter> selects submenus --->.         │
│ Highlighted letters are hotkeys.  Pressing <Y> includes, <N> excludes,│
│ <M> modularizes features.  Press <Esc><Esc> to exit, <?> for Help, </>│
│ for Search.  Legend: [*] built-in  [ ] excluded  <M> module  < >      │
│ ┌───────────────────────────────────────────────────────────────────┐ │
│ │    Generic Driver Options  --->                                  │ │
│ │    Connector - unified userspace <-> kernelspace linker  --->    │ │
│ │    Memory Technology Devices (MTD)  --->                         │ │
│ │    Parallel port support  --->                                   │ │
│ │    Plug and Play support  --->                                   │ │
│ │    Block devices  --->                                           │ │
│ │    ATA/ATAPI/MFM/RLL support  --->                               │ │
│ │    SCSI device support  --->                                     │ │
│ │    Multi-device support (RAID and LVM)  --->                     │ │
│ │    Fusion MPT device support  --->                               │ │
│ └───────────────────────────────────────────────────────────────────┘ │
│              <Select>    < Exit >    < Help >                         │
└───────────────────────────────────────────────────────────────────────┘
```

Figure 4-3. Device Drivers submenu

If the option is selected with Y, the angle brackets will contain a * character. If it is selected as a module with an M, they will contain an M character. If it is disabled with N, they will show only a blank space.

So, if you wish to change these three options to select only drivers that do not need external firmware at compile time, disable the option to prevent firmware from being built, and build the userspace firmware loader as a module, press Y for the first option, N for the second option, and M for the third, making the screen look like Figure 4-5.

After you are done with your changes to this screen, press either the Escape key or the right arrow followed by the Enter key to leave this submenu. All of the different kernel options can be explored in this manner.

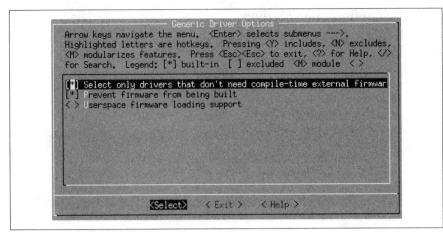

Figure 4-4. Generic Driver Options submenu

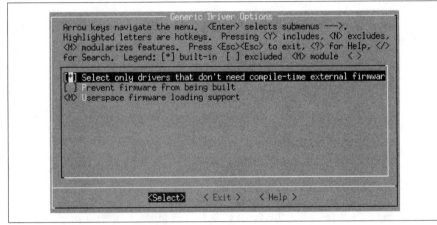

Figure 4-5. Generic Driver Options submenu changed

When you are finished making all of the changes you wish to make to the kernel configuration, exit the program by pressing the Escape key on the main menu. You will be shown the screen in Figure 4-6, asking whether you wish to save your changed kernel configuration.

Do you wish to save your new kernel configuration?

< Yes >   < No >

Figure 4-6. Saving kernel options

Press Enter to save the configuration, or if you wish to discard any changes made, press the right arrow to move to the <No> selection and then press Enter.

Graphical Configuration Methods

The *gconfig* and *xconfig* methods of configuring a kernel use a graphical program to allow you to modify the kernel configuration. The two methods are almost identical, the only difference being the different graphical toolkit with which they are written. *gconfig* is written using the GTK+ toolkit and has a two-pane screen looking like Figure 4-7.

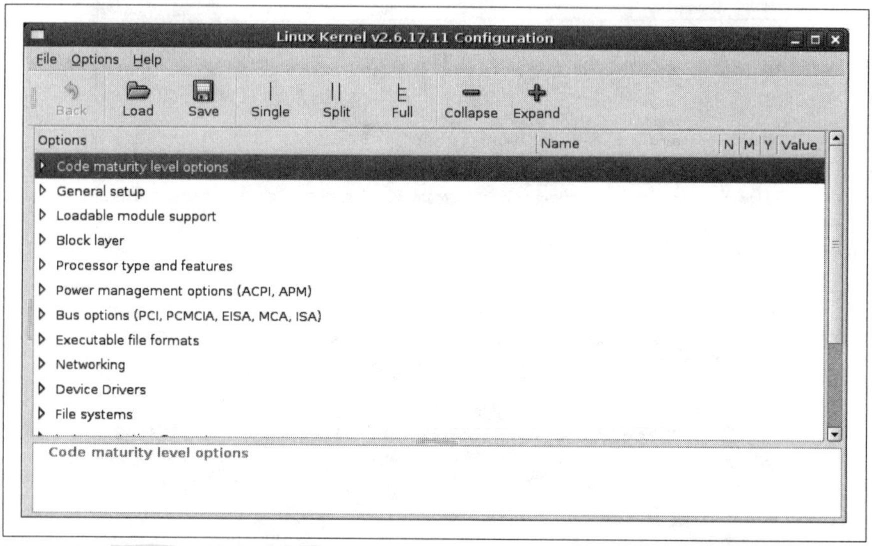

Figure 4-7. make gconfig screen

The *xconfig* method is written using the QT toolkit and has a three-pane screen looking like Figure 4-8.

Use the mouse to navigate the submenus and select options. For instance, you can use it in Figure 4-8 to select the Generic Driver Options submenu of the Device Drivers menu. This will change the *xconfig* screen to look like Figure 4-9. The corresponding *gconfig* screen is Figure 4-10.

Changing this submenu to disable the second option and make the third option be built as a module causes the screens to look like Figures 4-11 and 4-12.

Please note that in the *gconfig* method, a checked box signifies that the option will be built into the kernel, whereas a line though the box means the option will be built as a module. In the *xconfig* method, an option built as a module will be shown with a dot in the box.

Both of these methods prompt you to save your changed configuration when exiting the program, and offer the option to write that configuration out to a different file. In that way you can create multiple, differing configurations.

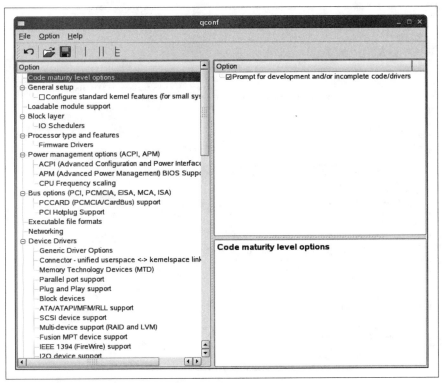

Figure 4-8. make xconfig screen

Building the Kernel

Now that you have created a kernel configuration that you wish to use, you need to build the kernel. This is as simple as entering a one-word command:

```
$ make
  CHK     include/linux/version.h
  UPD     include/linux/version.h
  SYMLINK include/asm -> include/asm-i386
  SPLIT   include/linux/autoconf.h -> include/config/*
  CC      arch/i386/kernel/asm-offsets.s
  GEN     include/asm-i386/asm-offsets.h
  CC      scripts/mod/empty.o
  HOSTCC  scripts/mod/mk_elfconfig
  MKELF   scripts/mod/elfconfig.h
  HOSTCC  scripts/mod/file2alias.o
  HOSTCC  scripts/mod/modpost.o
  HOSTCC  scripts/mod/sumversion.o
  HOSTLD  scripts/mod/modpost
  HOSTCC  scripts/kallsyms
  HOSTCC  scripts/conmakehash
  HOSTCC  scripts/bin2c
  CC      init/main.o
```

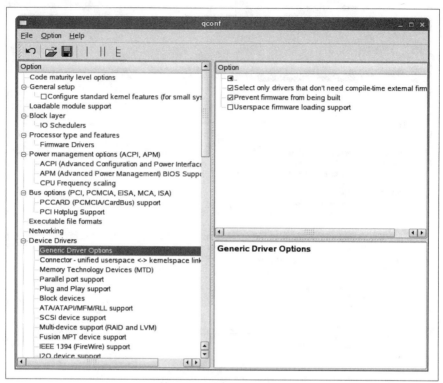

Figure 4-9. make xconfig Generic Driver Options

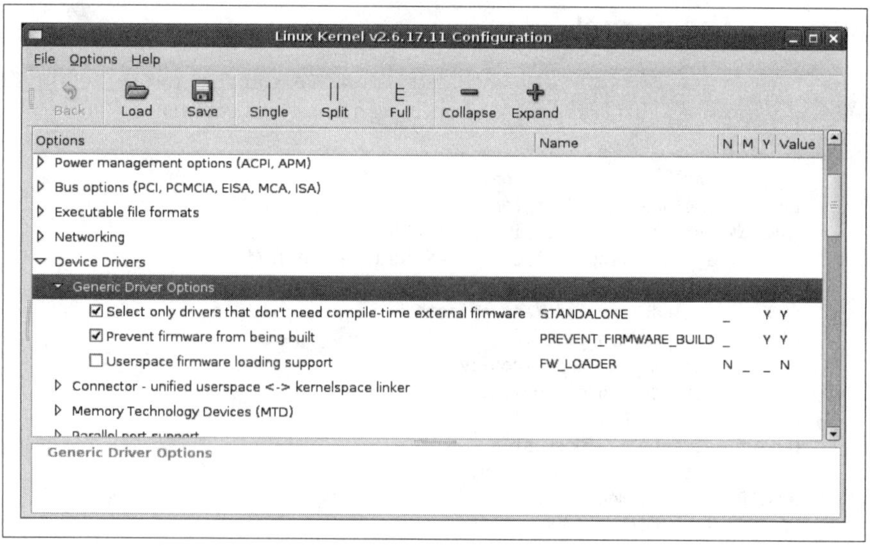

Figure 4-10. make gconfig Generic Driver Options

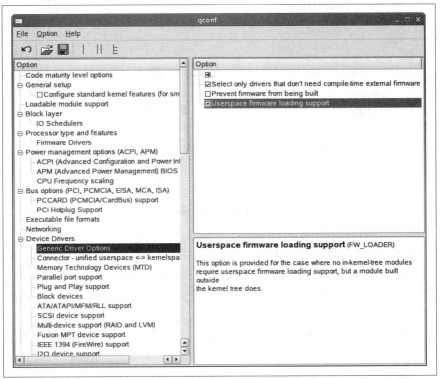

Figure 4-11. make xconfig Generic Driver Options changed

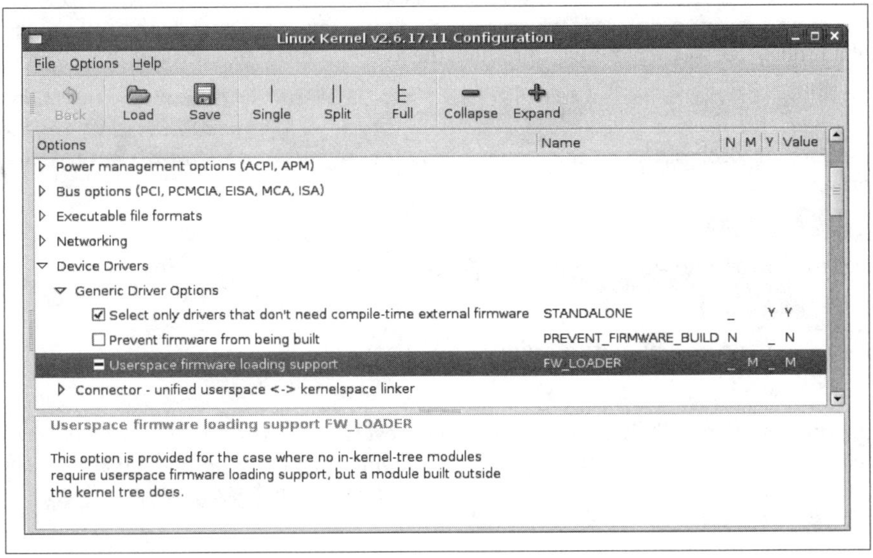

Figure 4-12. make gconfig Generic Driver Options changed

```
CHK    include/linux/compile.h
UPD    include/linux/compile.h
CC     init/version.o
CC     init/do_mounts.o
...
```

Running *make* causes the kernel build system to use the configuration you have selected to build a kernel and all modules needed to support that configuration.* While the kernel is building, *make* displays the individual filenames of what is currently happening, along with any build warnings or errors.

If the kernel build finished without any errors, you have successfully created a kernel image. However, it needs to be installed properly before you try to boot from it. See Chapter 5 for how to do this.

It is very unusual to get any build errors when building a released kernel version. If you do, please report them to the Linux kernel developers so they can be fixed.

Advanced Building Options

The kernel build system allows you to do many more things than just build the full kernel and modules. Chapter 10 includes the full list of options that the kernel build system provides. In this section, we will discuss some of these advanced build options. To see a full description of how to use other advanced build options, refer to the in-kernel documentation on the build system, which can be found in the *Documentation/kbuild* directory of the sources.

Building Faster on Multiprocessor Machines

The kernel build system works very well as a task that can be split up into little pieces and given to different processors. By doing this, you can use the full power of a multiprocessor machine and reduce the kernel build time considerably.

To build the kernel in a multithreaded way, use the *-j* option to the *make* program. It is best to give a number to the *-j* option that corresponds to twice the number of processors in the system. So, for a machine with two processors present, use:

```
$ make -j4
```

and for a machine with four processors, use:

```
$ make -j8
```

If you do not pass a numerical value to the *-j* option:

```
$ make -j
```

the build system will create a new thread for every subdirectory in the kernel tree, which can easily cause your machine to become unresponsive and take a much longer time to complete the build. Because of this, it is recommended that you always pass a number to the *-j* option.

---

* Older kernel versions prior to the 2.6 release required the additional step of *make modules* to build all needed kernel modules. That is no longer required.

Building Only a Portion of the Kernel

When doing kernel development, sometimes you wish to build only a specific subdirectory or a single file within the whole kernel tree. The kernel build system allows you to easily do this. To selectively build a specific directory, specify it on the build command line. For example, to build the files in the *drivers/usb/serial* directory, enter:

```
$ make drivers/usb/serial
```

Using this syntax, however, will not build the final module images in that directory. To do that, you can use the M= argument:

```
$ make M=drivers/usb/serial
```

which will build all the needed files in that directory and link the final module images.

When you build a single directory in one of the ways shown, the final kernel image is not relinked together. Therefore, any changes that were made to the subdirectories will not affect the final kernel image, which is probably not what you desire. Execute a final:

```
$ make
```

to have the build system check all changed object files and do the final kernel image link properly.

To build only a specific file in the kernel tree, just pass it as the argument to *make*. For example, if you wish to build only the *drivers/usb/serial/visor.ko* kernel module, enter:

```
$ make drivers/usb/serial/visor.ko
```

The build system will build all needed files for the *visor.ko* kernel module, and do the final link to create the module.

Source in One Place, Output in Another

Sometimes it is easier to have the source code for the kernel tree in a read-only location (such as on a CD-ROM, or in a source code control system), and place the output of the kernel build elsewhere, so that you do not disturb the original source tree. The kernel build system handles this easily, by requiring only the single argument O= to tell it where to place the output of the build. For example, if the kernel source is located on a CD-ROM mounted on */mnt/cdrom/* and you wish to place the built files in your local directory, enter:

```
$ cd /mnt/cdrom/linux-2.6.17.11
$ make O=~/linux/linux-2.6.17.11
```

All of the build files will be created in the *~/linux/linux-2.6.17.11/* directory. Please note that this O= option should also be passed to the configuration options of the build so that the configuration is correctly placed in the output directory and not in the directory containing the source code.

Different Architectures

A very useful feature is building the kernel in a cross-compiled manner to allow a more powerful machine to build a kernel for a smaller embedded system, or just to check a build for a different architecture to ensure that a change to the source code did not break something unexpected. The kernel build system allows you to specify a different architecture from the current system with the ARCH= argument. The build system also allows you to specify the specific compiler that you wish to use for the build by using the CC= argument or a cross-compile toolchain with the CROSS_COMPILE argument.

For example, to get the default kernel configuration of the x86_64 architecture, you would enter:

```
$ make ARCH=x86_64 defconfig
```

To build the whole kernel with an ARM toolchain located in */usr/local/bin/*, you would enter:

```
$ make ARCH=arm CROSS_COMPILE=/usr/local/bin/arm-linux-
```

It is useful even for a non-cross-compiled kernel to change what the build system uses for the compiler. Examples of this are using the *distcc* or *ccache* programs, both of which help greatly reduce the time it takes to build a kernel. To use the *ccache* program as part of the build system, enter:

```
$ make CC="ccache gcc"
```

To use both *distcc* and *ccache* together, enter:

```
$ make CC="ccache distcc"
```

5

Installing and Booting from a Kernel

Previous chapters showed you how to download and build your kernel. Now that you have an executable file—along with any modules you built—it is time to install the kernel and attempt to boot it. In this chapter, unlike earlier ones, all of the commands need to be run as the root user. This can be done by prefixing each command with *sudo*, by using the *su* command to become *root*, or actually by logging in as *root*.

To see whether you have *sudo* installed and the proper access set up, do the following:

```
$ sudo ls ~/linux/linux-2.6.17.11/Makefile
Password:
Makefile
```

Enter either your own password at the password prompt, or the password of the system administrator (root). The choice depends on how the *sudo* command is set up. If this is successful, and you see the line containing:

```
Makefile
```

then you can skip to the next section.

If *sudo* is not installed or giving you the proper rights, try using the *su* command:

```
$ su
Password:
# exit
exit
$
```

At the password prompt, enter the password of the system administrator (*root*). When the *su* program successfully accepts the password, you are transferred to running everything with full root privileges. Be very careful while as *root*, and do only the minimum needed; then exit the program to continue back as your normal user account.

Using a Distribution's Installation Scripts

Almost all distributions come with a script called *installkernel* that can be used by the kernel build system to automatically install a built kernel into the proper location and modify the bootloader so that nothing extra needs to be done by the developer.[*]

 Distributions that offer *installkernel* usually put it in a package called *mkinitrd*, so try to install that package if you cannot find the script on your machine.

If you have built any modules and want to use use this method to install a kernel, first enter:

```
# make modules_install
```

This will install all the modules that you have built and place them in the proper location in the filesystem for the new kernel to properly find. Modules are placed in the */lib/modules/kernel_version* directory, where *kernel_version* is the kernel version of the new kernel you have just built.

After the modules have been successfully installed, the main kernel image must be installed:

```
# make install
```

This will kick off the following process:

1. The kernel build system will verify that the kernel has been successfully built properly.

2. The build system will install the static kernel portion into the */boot* directory and name this executable file based on the kernel version of the built kernel.

3. Any needed initial ramdisk images will be automatically created, using the modules that have just been installed during the *modules_install* phase.

4. The bootloader program will be properly notified that a new kernel is present, and it will be added to the appropriate menu so the user can select it the next time the machine is booted.

5. After this is finished, the kernel is successfully installed, and you can safely reboot and try out your new kernel image. Note that this installation does not overwrite any older kernel images, so if there is a problem with your new kernel image, the old kernel can be selected at boot time.

---

[*] Notable exceptions to this rule are Gentoo and other "from scratch" types distributions, which expect users to know how to install kernels on their own. These types of distributions include documentation on how to install a new kernel, so consult it for the exact method required.

Installing by Hand

If your distribution does not have a *installkernel* command, or you wish to just do the work by hand to understand the steps involved, here they are:

The modules must be installed:

```
# make modules_install
```

The static kernel image must be copied into the */boot* directory. For an i386-based kernel, do the following:

```
# make kernelversion
2.6.17.11
```

Note that the kernel version will probably be different for your kernel. Use this value in place of the text KERNEL_VERSION in the following steps:

```
# cp arch/i386/boot/bzImage /boot/bzImage-KERNEL_VERSION
# cp System.map /boot/System.map-KERNEL_VERSION
```

Modify the bootloader so it knows about the new kernel. This involves editing a configuration file for the bootloader you use, and is covered later in "Modifying the Bootloader for the New Kernel" for the GRUB and LILO bootloaders.

If the boot process does not work properly, it's usually because an initial ramdisk image is needed. To create this properly, use the steps in the beginning of this chapter for installing a kernel automatically, because the distribution install scripts know how to properly create the ramdisk using the needed scripts and tools. Because each distribution does this differently, it is beyond the scope of this book to cover all of the different methods of building the ramdisk image.

Here is a handy script that can be used to install the kernel automatically instead of having to type the previous commands all the time:

```
#!/bin/sh
#
# installs a kernel
#
make modules_install

# find out what kernel version this is
for TAG in VERSION PATCHLEVEL SUBLEVEL EXTRAVERSION ; do
    eval `sed -ne "/^$TAG/s/ //gp" Makefile`
done
SRC_RELEASE=$VERSION.$PATCHLEVEL.$SUBLEVEL$EXTRAVERSION

# figure out the architecture
ARCH=`grep "CONFIG_ARCH " include/linux/autoconf.h | cut -f 2 -d "\""`

# copy the kernel image
cp arch/$ARCH/boot/bzImage /boot/bzImage-"$SRC_RELEASE"

# copy the System.map file
cp System.map /boot/System.map-"$SRC_RELEASE"

echo "Installed $SRC_RELEASE for $ARCH"
```

Modifying the Bootloader for the New Kernel

There are two common Linux kernel bootloaders: GRUB and LILO. GRUB is the one more commonly used in modern distributions, and does some things a little more easily than LILO, but LILO is still seen as well. We'll cover both in this section.

To determine which bootloader your system uses, look in the */boot/* directory. If there is a *grub* subdirectory:

```
$ ls -F /boot | grep grub
grub/
```

then you are using the GRUB program to boot with. If this directory is not present, look for the presence of the */etc/lilo.conf* file:

```
$ ls /etc/lilo.conf
/etc/lilo.conf
```

If this is present, you are using the LILO program to boot with.

The steps involved in adding a new kernel to each of these programs are different, so follow only the section that corresponds to the program you are using.

GRUB

To let GRUB know that a new kernel is present, all you need to do is modify the */boot/grub/menu.lst* file. For full details on the structure of this file, and all of the different options available, please see the GRUB info pages:

```
$ info grub
```

The easiest way to add a new kernel entry to the */boot/grub/menu.lst* file is to copy an existing entry. For example, consider the following *menu.lst* file from a Gentoo system:

```
timeout 300
default 0

splashimage=(hd0,0)/grub/splash.xpm.gz

title 2.6.16.11
    root (hd0,0)
    kernel /bzImage-2.6.16.11 root=/dev/sda2 vga=0x0305

title 2.6.16
    root (hd0,0)
    kernel /bzImage-2.6.16 root=/dev/sda2 vga=0x0305
```

The line starting with the word `title` defines a new kernel entry, so this file contains two entries. Simply copy one block of lines beginning with the `title` line, such as:

```
title 2.6.16.11
    root (hd0,0)
    kernel /bzImage-2.6.16.11 root=/dev/sda2 vga=0x0305
```

Then, add the block to the end of the file, and edit the version number to contain the version number of the new kernel you just installed. The title does not matter, so long as it is unique, but it is displayed in the boot menu, so you should make it something meaningful. In our example, we installed the 2.6.17.11 kernel, so the final copy of the file looks like:

```
timeout 300
default 0

splashimage=(hd0,0)/grub/splash.xpm.gz

title 2.6.16.11
    root (hd0,0)
    kernel /bzImage-2.6.16.11 root=/dev/sda2 vga=0x0305

title 2.6.16
    root (hd0,0)
    kernel /bzImage-2.6.16 root=/dev/sda2 vga=0x0305

title 2.6.17.11
    root (hd0,0)
    kernel /bzImage-2.6.17.11 root=/dev/sda2 vga=0x0305
```

After you save the file, reboot the system and ensure that the new kernel image's title comes up in the boot menu. Use the down arrow to highlight the new kernel version, and press Enter to boot the new kernel image.

LILO

To let LILO know that a new kernel is present, you must modify the */etc/lilo.conf* configuration file and then run the *lilo* command to apply the changes made to the configuration file. For full details on the structure of the LILO configuration file, please see the LILO manpage:

```
$ man lilo
```

The easiest way to add a new kernel entry to the */etc/lilo.conf* file is to copy an existing entry. For example, consider the following LILO configuration file from a Gentoo system:

```
boot=/dev/hda
prompt
timeout=50
default=2.6.12

image=/boot/bzImage-2.6.15
    label=2.6.15
    read-only
    root=/dev/hda2

image=/boot/bzImage-2.6.12
    label=2.6.12
    read-only
    root=/dev/hda2
```

The line starting with the word image= defines a new kernel entry, so this file contains two entries. Simply copy one block of lines beginning with image=, such as:

```
image=/boot/bzImage-2.6.15
    label=2.6.15
    read-only
    root=/dev/hda2
```

Then, add the block to the end of the file, and edit the version number to contain the version number of the new kernel you just installed. The label does not matter, so long as it is unique, but it is displayed in the boot menu, so you should make it something meaningful. In our example, we installed the 2.6.17.11 kernel, so the final copy of the file looks like:

```
boot=/dev/hda
prompt
timeout=50
default=2.6.12

image=/boot/bzImage-2.6.15
    label=2.6.15
    read-only
    root=/dev/hda2

image=/boot/bzImage-2.6.12
    label=2.6.12
    read-only
    root=/dev/hda2

image=/boot/bzImage-2.6.17
    label=2.6.17
    read-only
    root=/dev/hda2
```

After you save the file, run the */sbin/lilo* program to write the configuration changes out to the boot section of the disk:

```
# /sbin/lilo
```

Now the system can be safely rebooted. The new kernel choice can be seen in the list of kernels that are available at boot time. Use the down arrow to highlight the new kernel version, and press Enter to boot the new kernel image.

6

Upgrading a Kernel

Inevitably it happens: you have a custom-built kernel, working just wonderfully except for one little thing that you know is fixed in the latest release from the kernel developers. Or a security problem is found, and a new stable kernel release is made public. Either way, you are faced with the issue of upgrading the kernel and you do not want to lose all the time and effort that went into making that perfect kernel configuration.

This chapter is going to show how easy it is to update a kernel from an older versions, while still retaining all of the configuration options from the previous one.

First off, please back up the .config file in the kernel source directory. You have spent some time and effort into creating it, and it should be saved in case something goes wrong when trying to upgrade.

```
$ cd ~/linux/linux-2.6.17.11
$ cp .config ../good_config
```

Only five simple steps are needed to upgrade a kernel from a previously built one:

1. Get the new source code.
2. Apply the changes to the old source tree to bring it up to the newer level.
3. Reconfigure the kernel based on the previous kernel configuration.
4. Build the new kernel.
5. Install the new kernel.

The last two steps work the same as described before, so we will only discuss the first three steps in this chapter.

In this chapter, we are going to assume that you have built a successful 2.6.17.9 kernel release, and want to upgrade to the 2.6.17.11 release.

Download the New Source

The Linux kernel developers realize that users do not wish to download the entire source code to the kernel for every update. That would be a waste of bandwidth and time. Because of this, they offer a patch that can upgrade an older kernel release to a newer one.[*]

On the main *kernel.org* web site, you will remember that it contained a list of the current kernel versions that are available for download, as shown in Figure 6-1.

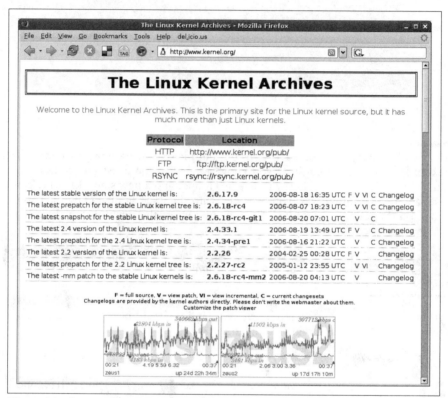

Figure 6-1. The main kernel.org web site

Previously, you used the link pointed to you by the F to download the entire source code for the kernel. However, if you click on the name of the kernel release, it will download a patch file instead, as shown in Figure 6-2.

---

[*] It is called *patch* because the program *patch* takes the file and applies it to the original tree, creating the new tree. The patch file contains a representation of the changes that are necessary to reconstruct the new files, based on the old ones. Patch files are readable, and contain a list of the lines that are to be removed and the lines that are to be added, with some context within the file showing where the changes should be made.

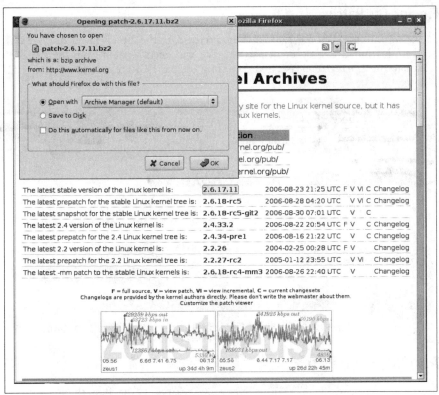

Figure 6-2. Downloading a patch from kernel.org

This is what we want to do when upgrading. But we need to figure out what patch to download.

Which Patch Applies to Which Release?

A kernel patch file will upgrade the source code from only one specific release to another specific release. Here is how the different patch files can be applied:

- Stable kernel patches apply to the base kernel version. This means that the 2.6.17.10 patch will only apply to the 2.6.17 kernel release. The 2.6.17.10 kernel patch will not apply to the 2.6.17.9 kernel or any other release.

- Base kernel release patches only apply to the previous base kernel version. This means that the 2.6.18 patch will only apply to the 2.6.17 kernel release. It will not apply to the last 2.6.17.y kernel release, or any other release.

- Incremental patches upgrade from a specific release to the next release. This allows developers to not have to downgrade their kernel and then upgrade it, just to switch from the latest stable release to the next stable release (remember that the stable release patches are only against the base kernel, not the previous stable release). Whenever possible, it is recommended that you use the incremental patches to make your life easier.

Finding the Patch

As we want to go from the 2.6.17.9 kernel release, to the 2.6.17.11 release, we will need to download two different patches. We will need a patch from the 2.6.17.9 release to the 2.6.17.10 release, and then from the 2.6.17.10 release to the 2.6.17.11 release.*

The stable and base kernel patches are located in the same directory structure as the main source trees. All incremental patches can be found one level lower, in the *incr* subdirectory. So, to find the patch that goes from 2.6.17.9 to 2.6.17.10, we look in the */pub/linux/kernel/v2.6/incr* directory to find the files we need:†

```
$ cd ~/linux
$ lftp ftp.kernel.org/pub/linux/kernel/v2.6/incr
cd ok, cwd=/pub/linux/kernel/v2.6/incr
lftp ftp.kernel.org:/pub/linux/kernel/v2.6/incr> ls *2.6.17.9*.bz2
-rw-rw-r--    1 536        536            2872 Aug 22 19:23 patch-2.6.17.9-10.
bz2
lftp ftp.kernel.org:/pub/linux/kernel/v2.6/incr> get patch-2.6.17.9-10.bz2
2872 bytes transferred
lftp ftp.kernel.org:/pub/linux/kernel/v2.6/incr> get patch-2.6.17.10-11.bz2
7901 bytes transferred
lftp ftp.kernel.org:/pub/linux/kernel/v2.6/incr> exit
$ ls -F
good_config linux-2.6.17.9/ patch-2.6.17.10-11.bz2  patch-2.6.17.9-10.bz2
```

Applying the Patch

As the patches we have downloaded are compressed, the first thing to do is uncompress them with the *bzip2* command:

```
$ bzip2 -dv patch-2.6.17.9-10.bz2
  patch-2.6.17.9-10.bz2: done
$ bzip2 -dv patch-2.6.17.10-11.bz2
  patch-2.6.17.10-11.bz2: done
$ ls -F
good_config linux-2.6.17.9/  patch-2.6.17.10-11  patch-2.6.17.9-10
```

Now we need to apply the patch files to the kernel directory. Go into the directory:

```
$ cd linux-2.6.17.9
```

Now run the *patch* program to apply the first patch moving the source tree from the 2.6.17.9 to the 2.6.17.10 release:

```
$ patch -p1 < ../patch-2.6.17.9-10
```

---

* If you need to upgrade more than two versions, it is recommended as a way to save steps, to go backward and then upgrade forward. In this case, we could go backward from 2.6.17.9 to 2.6.17 and then forward from 2.6.17 to 2.6.17.11.

† In this example, we use the very good *lftp* FTP program to download the patch files. Any FTP program or a web browser can be used to download the same files. The important thing here is to show where the files are located.

```
patching file Makefile
patching file block/elevator.c
patching file fs/udf/super.c
patching file fs/udf/truncate.c
patching file include/net/sctp/sctp.h
patching file include/net/sctp/sm.h
patching file net/sctp/sm_make_chunk.c
patching file net/sctp/sm_statefuns.c
patching file net/sctp/socket.c
```

Verify that the patch really did work properly and that there are no errors or warnings in the output of the patch program. It is also a good idea to look at the *Makefile* of the kernel to see the kernel version:

```
$ head -n 5 Makefile
VERSION = 2
PATCHLEVEL = 6
SUBLEVEL = 17
EXTRAVERSION = .10
NAME=Crazed Snow-Weasel
```

Now that the kernel is at the 2.6.17.10 release level, do the same thing as before, and apply the patch to bring it up to the 2.6.17.11 level:

```
$ patch -p1 < ../patch-2.6.17.10-11
patching file Makefile
patching file arch/ia64/kernel/sys_ia64.c
patching file arch/sparc/kernel/sys_sparc.c
patching file arch/sparc64/kernel/sys_sparc.c
patching file drivers/char/tpm/tpm_tis.c
patching file drivers/ieee1394/ohci1394.c
patching file drivers/md/dm-mpath.c
patching file drivers/md/raid1.c
patching file drivers/net/sky2.c
patching file drivers/pci/quirks.c
patching file drivers/serial/Kconfig
patching file fs/befs/linuxvfs.c
patching file fs/ext3/super.c
patching file include/asm-generic/mman.h
patching file include/asm-ia64/mman.h
patching file include/asm-sparc/mman.h
patching file include/asm-sparc64/mman.h
patching file kernel/timer.c
patching file lib/spinlock_debug.c
patching file mm/mmap.c
patching file mm/swapfile.c
patching file net/bridge/netfilter/ebt_ulog.c
patching file net/core/dst.c
patching file net/core/rtnetlink.c
patching file net/ipv4/fib_semantics.c
patching file net/ipv4/netfilter/arp_tables.c
patching file net/ipv4/netfilter/ip_tables.c
patching file net/ipv4/netfilter/ipt_ULOG.c
patching file net/ipv4/route.c
patching file net/ipx/af_ipx.c
patching file net/netfilter/nfnetlink_log.c
```

Again verify that the output of the patch program did not show any errors and look at the *Makefile*:

```
$ head -n 5 Makefile
VERSION = 2
PATCHLEVEL = 6
SUBLEVEL = 17
EXTRAVERSION = .11
NAME=Crazed Snow-Weasel
```

Now that the source code is successfully updated to the version you wish to use, it is a good idea to go back and change the directory name to refer to the kernel version number to avoid confusion at a later time:

```
$ cd ..
$ mv linux-2.6.17.9 linux-2.6.17.11
$ ls -F
good_config  linux-2.6.17.11/  patch-2.6.17.10-11  patch-2.6.17.9-10
```

Reconfigure the Kernel

Previously, we used the *make menuconfig* or *gconfig* or *xconfig* method to change different configuration options. But once you have a working configuration, the only thing that is necessary is to update it with any new options that have been added to the kernel since the last release. To do this, the *make oldconfig* and *make silentoldconfig* options should be used.

make oldconfig takes the current kernel configuration in the *.config* file, and updates it based on the new kernel release. To do this, it prints out all configuration questions, and provides an answer for them if the option is already handled in the configuration file. If there is a new option, the program stops and asks the user what the new configuration value should be set to. After answering the prompt, the program continues on until the whole kernel configuration is finished.

make silentoldconfig works exactly the same way as *oldconfig*, but it does not print anything to the screen, unless it needs to ask a question about a new configuration option.

Usually, when upgrading between different versions of the stable releases, no new configuration options are added, as this is supposed to be a stable kernel series. If this happens, there are no new questions that need to be answered for the kernel configuration, so the program continues successfully without any need for user intervention. An example of this is moving from the 2.6.17.9 to 2.6.17.11 release:

```
$ cd linux-2.6.17.11
$ make silentoldconfig
scripts/kconfig/conf -s arch/i386/Kconfig
#
# using defaults found in .config
#
```

The following example shows what happens when a new kernel option shows up in a new release. The kernel option to enable *Mutex debugging* is a new one for certain kernel releases. Here is the output when this happened:

```
$ make silentoldconfig
scripts/kconfig/conf -s arch/i386/Kconfig
#
# using defaults found in .config
#
*
* Restart config...
*
*
* Kernel hacking
*
Show timing information on printks (PRINTK_TIME) [Y/n/?] y
Magic SysRq key (MAGIC_SYSRQ) [Y/n/?] y
Kernel debugging (DEBUG_KERNEL) [Y/n/?] y
   Kernel log buffer size (16 => 64KB, 17 => 128KB) (LOG_BUF_SHIFT) [16] 16
   Detect Soft Lockups (DETECT_SOFTLOCKUP) [Y/n/?] y
   Collect scheduler statistics (SCHEDSTATS) [N/y/?] n
   Debug slab memory allocations (DEBUG_SLAB) [Y/n/?] y
      Memory leak debugging (DEBUG_SLAB_LEAK) [Y/n] y
   Mutex debugging, deadlock detection (DEBUG_MUTEXES) [N/y/?] (NEW) y
```

The configuration program stops at this option and asks for the user to choose an option. Press y, and the program continues on:

```
   Spinlock debugging (DEBUG_SPINLOCK) [Y/n/?] y
   Sleep-inside-spinlock checking (DEBUG_SPINLOCK_SLEEP) [Y/n/?] y
   kobject debugging (DEBUG_KOBJECT) [N/y/?] n
   Highmem debugging (DEBUG_HIGHMEM) [N/y/?] n
   Compile the kernel with debug info (DEBUG_INFO) [N/y/?] n
Debug Filesystem (DEBUG_FS) [Y/?] y
Debug VM (DEBUG_VM) [N/y/?] n
Compile the kernel with frame pointers (FRAME_POINTER) [N/y/?] n
Compile the kernel with frame unwind information (UNWIND_INFO) [N/y/?] n
Force gcc to inline functions marked 'inline' (FORCED_INLINING) [N/y/?] n
torture tests for RCU (RCU_TORTURE_TEST) [N/m/y/?] n
Check for stack overflows (DEBUG_STACKOVERFLOW) [N/y/?] n
Stack utilization instrumentation (DEBUG_STACK_USAGE) [N/y/?] n
Stack backtraces per line (STACK_BACKTRACE_COLS) [2] 2
*
* Page alloc debug is incompatible with Software Suspend on i386
*
Write protect kernel read-only data structures (DEBUG_RODATA) [N/y/?] n
Use 4Kb for kernel stacks instead of 8Kb (4KSTACKS) [N/y/?] n
```

So upgrading the kernel configuration for a new release is as simple as using a different configuration option to *make*. With this method, you do not need to use the graphical or text-oriented configuration programs for any new kernel update.

Can't This Be Automated?

The whole process of downloading the proper patch file, uncompressing it, and then applying it seems to be ripe for automating. Kernel developers being the type that like to automate repetitive tasks, the program *ketchup* has been created to handle all of this automatically. See Appendix A for more details on how this program works and how to use it.

II

Major Customizations

This part explains the most common customizations that Linux users perform, and useful combinations of options to customize.

43

7

Customizing a Kernel

One of the hardest parts of building your own version of the Linux kernel is determining exactly which drivers and configuration options are needed for your machine to work properly. This chapter will walk you through this process of finding and selecting the correct drivers.

Using a Distribution Kernel

One of the easiest ways to determine which modules are necessary is to start with the kernel configuration that comes with your distribution's kernel package. It is also much easier to determine which drivers are needed on a running system, where the proper drivers are already bound to the hardware.

If you do not already have a Linux distribution installed on the machine that you are building the kernel for, use a LiveCD version of a distribution. This allows you to boot Linux on the machine and determine what kernel configuration options are needed in order to get the hardware working properly.

Where Is the Kernel Configuration?

Almost all distributions provide the kernel configuration files as part of the distribution kernel package. Read the distribution-specific documentation for how to find these configurations. It is usually somewhere below the */usr/src/linux/* directory tree.

If the kernel configuration is hard to find, look in the kernel itself. Most distribution kernels are built to include the configuration within the */proc* filesystem. To determine if this is true for your running kernel, enter:

```
$ ls /proc/config.gz
/proc/config.gz
```

If the */proc/config.gz* filename is present, copy this file to your kernel source directory and uncompress it:

```
$ cp /proc/config.gz ~/linux/
$ cd ~/linux
$ gzip -dv config.gz
config.gz:       74.9% -- replaced with config
```

Copy this configuration file into your kernel directory and rename it to *.config*. Then use it as the basis of the kernel configuration to build the kernel as described in Chapter 4.

Using this configuration file should always generate a working kernel image for your machine. The disadvantage of this kernel image is that you will have built almost every kernel module and driver that is present in the kernel source tree. This is almost never needed for a single machine, so you can start to turn off different drivers and options that are not needed. It is recommended that you disable only those options that you are sure you do not need, as there might be parts of the system that rely on specific options being enabled.

Finding Which Module Is Needed

A configuration file that comes from a distribution takes a very long time to build, because of all of the different drivers being built. You want to build only the drivers for the hardware that you have, which will save time on building the kernel, and allows you to build some or all of the drivers into the kernel itself, possibly saving a bit of memory, and on some architectures, making for a faster running system. To cut your drivers down, you need to determine which modules are needed to drive your hardware. We will walk though two examples of how to find out what driver is needed to control what piece of hardware.

Several locations on your system store useful information for determining which devices are bound to which drivers in a running kernel. The most important location is a virtual filesystem called *sysfs*. *sysfs* should always be mounted at the */sys* location in your filesystem by the initialization scripts of your Linux distribution. *sysfs* provides a glimpse into how the different portions of the kernel are hooked together, with many different symlinks pointing all around the filesystem.

In all of the following examples, real *sysfs* paths and hardware types are shown. Your machine will be different, but the relative locations of information will be the same. Do not be alarmed if the filenames in *sysfs* are different from your machine; it is to be expected.

Additionally, the internal structure of the *sysfs* filesystem constantly changes around, due to the reorganization of devices and rethinking by the kernel developers about how to best display internal kernel structures to userspace. Because of this, over time, some of the symlinks previously mentioned in this chapter might not be present. However, the information is all still there, just moved around a little bit.

Example: Determining the network driver

One of the most common and important devices in the system is the network interface card. It is imperative to figure out which driver is controlling this device and enable it in your kernel configuration so that networking works properly.

First, work backward from the network connection name to find out which PCI device is controlling it. To do this, look at the different network names:

```
$ ls /sys/class/net/
eth0  eth1  eth2  lo
```

The *lo* directory represents the network loopback device, and is not attached to any real network device. The *eth0*, *eth1*, and *eth2* directories are what you should pay attention to, as they represent real network devices.

To look further at these network devices in order to figure out which you care about, use the *ifconfig* utility:

```
$ /sbin/ifconfig -a
eth0      Link encap:Ethernet  HWaddr 00:12:3F:65:7D:C2
          inet addr:192.168.0.13  Bcast:192.168.0.255  Mask:255.255.255.0
          UP BROADCAST NOTRAILERS RUNNING MULTICAST  MTU:1500  Metric:1
          RX packets:2720792 errors:0 dropped:0 overruns:0 frame:0
          TX packets:1815488 errors:0 dropped:0 overruns:0 carrier:0
          collisions:0 txqueuelen:100
          RX bytes:3103826486 (2960.0 Mb)  TX bytes:371424066 (354.2 Mb)
          Base address:0xdcc0 Memory:dfee0000-dff00000
eth1      Link encap:UNSPEC  HWaddr 80-65-00-12-7D-C2-3F-00-00-00-00-00-00-
          00-00-00
          BROADCAST MULTICAST  MTU:1500  Metric:1
          RX packets:0 errors:0 dropped:0 overruns:0 frame:0
          TX packets:0 errors:0 dropped:0 overruns:0 carrier:0
          collisions:0 txqueuelen:1000
          RX bytes:0 (0.0 b)  TX bytes:0 (0.0 b)
eth2      Link encap:UNSPEC  HWaddr 00-02-3C-04-11-09-D2-BA-00-00-00-00-00-
          00-00-00
          BROADCAST MULTICAST  MTU:1500  Metric:1
          RX packets:0 errors:0 dropped:0 overruns:0 frame:0
          TX packets:0 errors:0 dropped:0 overruns:0 carrier:0
          collisions:0 txqueuelen:1000
          RX bytes:0 (0.0 b)  TX bytes:0 (0.0 b)
lo        Link encap:Local Loopback
          inet addr:127.0.0.1  Mask:255.0.0.0
          UP LOOPBACK RUNNING  MTU:16436  Metric:1
          RX packets:60 errors:0 dropped:0 overruns:0 frame:0
          TX packets:60 errors:0 dropped:0 overruns:0 carrier:0
          collisions:0 txqueuelen:0
          RX bytes:13409 (13.0 Kb)  TX bytes:13409 (13.0 Kb)
```

From this list, you can tell that the eth0 device is the network device that is active and working, as can be seen by the lines:

```
eth0      Link encap:Ethernet  HWaddr 00:12:3F:65:7D:C2
          inet addr:192.168.0.13  Bcast:192.168.0.255  Mask:255.255.255.0
```

The ouput shows this is an Ethernet device with valid IP (inet) address assigned to it.

Now that we have determined that we want to make sure the eth0 device will be working in our new kernel, we need to find which driver is controlling it. This is simply a matter of walking the different links in the *sysfs* filesystem, which can be done in a one-line command:

```
$ basename `readlink /sys/class/net/eth0/device/driver/module`
e1000
```

The output shows that the module named e1000 is controlling the eth0 network device. The *basename* command shown compresses the following steps into a single command line:

1. Follow the */sys/class/net/eth0/device* symlink into the directory within the */sys/device/* tree that contains the information for the device that controls *eth0*. Note that the */sys/class/net/eth0* directory might also be a symlink on the newer versions of the kernel.

2. Within the directory that describes the device in *sysfs*, there is a symlink to the driver bound to this device. That symlink is called *driver*, so we follow that link.

3. Within the directory that describes the driver in *sysfs*, there is a symlink to the module that this driver is contained within. That symlink is called module. We want the target of that symlink. To get the target, we use the *readlink* command, which produces output such as:

   ```
   $ readlink /sys/class/net/eth0/device/driver/module
   ../../../../module/e1000
   ```

4. Because we care only about the name of the module, we want to strip the rest of the path off the output of the *readlink* command, and only save the right-most portion. That is what the *basename* command does. Executed directly on a pathname, it would produce:

   ```
   $ basename ../../../../module/e1000
   e1000
   ```

So we put the output of the long symlink traversal to the *readlink* location into the *basename* program, enabling the whole process to be done in one line.

Now that we have the module name, we need to find the kernel configuration option that controls it. You can look through the different network device configuration menus or search the kernel source code itself to make sure you have the right option:

```
$ cd ~/linux/linux-2.6.17.8
$ find -type f -name Makefile | xargs grep e1000
./drivers/net/Makefile:obj-$(CONFIG_E1000) += e1000/
./drivers/net/e1000/Makefile:obj-$(CONFIG_E1000) += e1000.o
./drivers/net/e1000/Makefile:e1000-objs := e1000_main.o e1000_hw.o e1000_
ethtool.o e1000_param.o
```

Remember to replace the **e1000** used for this example with the name of the module that you are looking to find.

The important thing to look for in the output of the previous *find* command is any line that has the term CONFIG_ in it. That is the configuration option that the kernel needs to have enabled in order to build the module. In the above example, the option CONFIG_E1000 is the configuration option that you are looking for.

Now you have the information you need to configure the kernel. Run the menu configuration tool:

```
$ make menuconfig
```

Then press the / key (which initiates a search) and type in the configuration option, minus the CONFIG_ portion of the string. This process is shown in Figure 7-1.

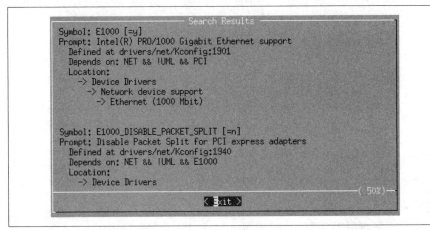

Figure 7-1. Searching in menuconfig

The kernel configuration system will then tell you exactly where to select the option to enable this module. See Figure 7-2.

```
———————————————————— Search Results ————————————————————
Symbol: E1000 [=y]
Prompt: Intel(R) PRO/1000 Gigabit Ethernet support
  Defined at drivers/net/Kconfig:1901
  Depends on: NET && !UML && PCI
  Location:
    -> Device Drivers
      -> Network device support
        -> Ethernet (1000 Mbit)

Symbol: E1000_DISABLE_PACKET_SPLIT [=n]
Prompt: Disable Packet Split for PCI express adapters
  Defined at drivers/net/Kconfig:1940
  Depends on: NET && !UML && E1000
  Location:
    -> Device Drivers
                                                        ( 50%)—
                         < Exit >
```

Figure 7-2. Result of searching in menuconfig

The first item in the display exactly matches what you searched for. The location information in the display tells you that to build the module E1000 into the kernel, and the following configuration option must be enabled:

```
Device Drivers
    Network device support
        [*] Network device support
```

Customizing a Kernel

```
    Ethernet (1000 Mbit)
[*] Intel(R) PRO/1000 Gigabit Ethernet support
```

These steps will work for any type of device active in the kernel.

Example: A USB device

As another example, let's look at a USB-to-serial converter that is present in our example system. It is currently connected to the */dev/ttyUSB0* port, so you need to look in the *sysfs* tty section:

```
$ ls /sys/class/tty/ | grep USB
ttyUSB0
```

You can trace through *sysfs* for this device to find the controlling module, as shown in the previous section:

```
$ basename `readlink /sys/class/tty/ttyUSB0/device/driver/module`
pl2303
```

Then search the kernel source tree to find the configuration option that you need to enable:

```
$ cd ~/linux/linux-2.6.17.8
$ find -type f -name Makefile | xargs grep pl2303
./drivers/usb/serial/Makefile:obj-$(CONFIG_USB_SERIAL_PL2303) += pl2303.o
```

Use the kernel configuration tool, as shown in Figure 7-3, to find the proper option to enable in order to set the CONFIG_USB_SERIAL_PL2303 option.

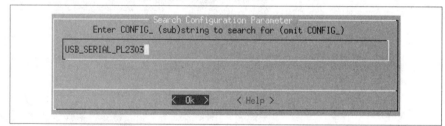

Figure 7-3. Searching for USB_SERIAL_PL2303

In our case, this displays the screen shown in Figure 7-4.

This shows exactly where to find the USB Prolific 2303 Single Port Serial Driver option that is needed to control this device properly.

Summary of device discovery

In summary, here are the steps needed to find the driver for a device that has a working driver already bound to it:

1. Find the proper *sysfs* class device that the device is bound to. Network devices are listed in */sys/class/net* and tty devices in */sys/class/tty*. Other types of devices are listed in other directories in */sys/class*, depending on the type of device.

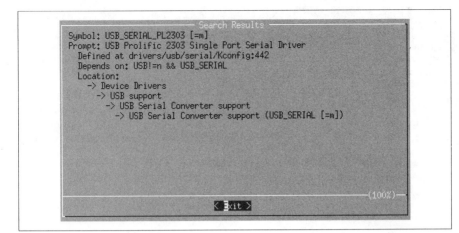

Figure 7-4. Result of searching for USB_SERIAL_PL2303

2. Trace through the *sysfs* tree to find the module name that controls this device. It will be found in the */sys/class/class_name/device_name/device/driver/module*, and can be displayed using the *readlink* and *basename* applications:

```
$ basename `readlink /sys/class/class_name/device_name/device/driver/
module`
```

3. Search the kernel Makefiles for the CONFIG_ rule that builds this module name by using *find* and *grep*:

```
$ find -type f -name Makefile | xargs grep module_name
```

4. Search in the kernel configuration system for that configuration value and go to the location in the menu that it specifies to enable that driver to be built.

Let the kernel tell us what we need

Now that we have gone through all of the steps of poking around in *sysfs* and following symlinks to module names, here is a very simple script that will do all of that work, in a different way:

```
#!/bin/bash
#
# find_all_modules.sh
#
for i in `find /sys/ -name modalias -exec cat {} \;`; do
    /sbin/modprobe --config /dev/null --show-depends $i ;
done | rev | cut -f 1 -d '/' | rev | sort -u
```

You can download an example file containing this script from the book's web site, provided in the "How to Contact Us" section of the Preface.

This script goes through *sysfs* and finds all files called *modalias*. The *modalias* file contains the module alias that tells the *modprobe* command which module should be loaded to control this device. The module alias is made up of a combination of device manufacturer, ID, class type, and other unique identifiers for that specific type of device. All kernel driver modules have an internal list of devices that they support that is generated automatically by the list of devices the driver tells the kernel it supports. The *modprobe* looks through this list of devices by all drivers and tries to match it up with the alias it has. If it finds a match, it will then load the module (this procedure is how the automatic driver loading functionality in Linux works).

The script has the *modprobe* program stop before actually loading the module, and just print out what actions it would take. This gives us a list of all of the modules that are needed to control all devices in the system. A little cleaning up of the list, by sorting it and finding the proper field to display, results in this output:

```
$ find_all_modules.sh
8139cp.ko
8139too.ko
ehci-hcd.ko
firmware_class.ko
i2c-i801.ko
ieee80211.ko
ieee80211_crypt.ko
ipw2200.ko
mii.ko
mmc_core.ko
pcmcia_core.ko
rsrc_nonstatic.ko
sdhci.ko
snd-hda-codec.ko
snd-hda-intel.ko
snd-page-alloc.ko
snd-pcm.ko
snd-timer.ko
snd.ko
soundcore.ko
uhci-hcd.ko
usbcore.ko
yenta_socket.ko
```

This is a list of all of the modules that are needed to control the hardware in the machine.

The script will also probably print out some error messages that look like:

```
FATAL: Module pci:v00008086d00002592sv000010CFsd000012E2bc03sc00i00 not
found.
FATAL: Module serio:ty01pr00id00ex00 not found.
```

Which means that it could not find a module that can control that device. Do not be concerned about this, as some devices do not have kernel drivers that will work for them.

Determining the Correct Module from Scratch

Sometimes you do not have the option of getting a distribution kernel working on a machine in order to determine what kernel modules are needed to drive the hardware. Or you have added new hardware to your system, and you need to figure out what kernel configuration option needs to be enabled to get it to work properly. This section will help you determine how to find that configuration option to get the hardware up and running.

The easiest way to figure out which driver controls a new device is to build all of the different drivers of that type in the kernel source tree as modules, and let the *udev* startup process match the driver to the device. Once this happens, you should be able to work backwards using the steps just discussed to determine the proper driver needed, and then go back and enable just that driver in the kernel configuration.

But if you do not want to build all drivers, or this does not work for some reason, it will require a bit more work to determine the proper driver that is needed. The following steps are complex and require digging in the kernel source code at times. Do not be afraid of this; it will only help you understand your hardware and the kernel source better.

The steps involved in matching the driver to the device differ depending on the type of device that you are working with. We will discuss the two most common forms of devices in this chapter: PCI and USB devices. The methods described here will also work with other types of devices.

Also, it is very important for the kernel to be able to find all of the filesystems in the system, the most important one being the root filesystem. We will go into how to do this later in "Root Filesystem."

PCI Devices

PCI devices are distinguished by vendor ID and device ID; each combination of vendor and device ID could require a unique driver. This is the basis for the research this section shows you.

For this example, let's use a PCI network card that is not working with the currently running kernel version. This example will be different from your situation, with different PCI device and bus ID values, but the steps involved should be relevant to any type of PCI device you wish to find a working driver for.

First, find the PCI device in the system that is not working. To get a list of all PCI devices, use the *lspci* program. Because we care only about Ethernet PCI devices, we will narrow our search of the PCI devices by searching only for strings containing the term Ethernet (case-insensitive):

```
$ /usr/sbin/lspci | grep -i ethernet
06:04.0 Ethernet controller: Realtek Semiconductor Co., Ltd.  RTL-8139/
8139C/8139C+ (rev 10)
```

This is the device we wish to get working.*

---

* Note that you can just try searching through the kernel configuration for a device that matches the string described here, a device from Realtek Semiconductor with a product name of RTL-8139/8139C/8139C+, but this does not always work. That is why we are taking the long way around in this chapter.

Almost all distributions place the *lspci* program in the */usr/sbin/* directory, but some place it in other locations. To find out where it is located, enter:

```
$ which lspci
/usr/sbin/lspci
```

If you are using a distribution that puts it somewhere else, please use that path whenever we discuss using *lspci*.

The first few bits of the *lspci* output show the PCI bus ID for this device, 06:04.0. That is the value we will use when looking through *sysfs* in order to find out more information about this device.

Go into *sysfs* where all of the different PCI devices are listed, and look at their names:

```
$ cd /sys/bus/pci/devices/
$ ls
0000:00:00.0   0000:00:1d.0   0000:00:1e.0   0000:00:1f.3   0000:06:03.3
0000:00:02.0   0000:00:1d.1   0000:00:1f.0   0000:06:03.0   0000:06:03.4
0000:00:02.1   0000:00:1d.2   0000:00:1f.1   0000:06:03.1   0000:06:04.0
0000:00:1b.0   0000:00:1d.7   0000:00:1f.2   0000:06:03.2   0000:06:05.0
```

The kernel numbers PCI devices with a leading 0000: that do not show up in the output of the *lspci* program.* So add the leading 0000: onto the number that you found using *lspci* and go into that directory:

```
$ cd 0000:06:04.0
```

In this directory, you want to know the values of the *vendor* and *device* filenames:

```
$ cat vendor
0x10ec
$ cat device
0x8139
```

These are the vendor and device IDs for this PCI device. The kernel uses these values to match a driver to a device properly. PCI drivers tell the kernel which vendor and device IDs they will support so that the kernel knows how to bind the driver to the proper device. Write them down somewhere, as we will refer to them later.

Now that we know the vendor and product ID for this PCI device, we need to find the proper kernel driver that advertises that it supports this device. Go back to the kernel source directory:

```
$ cd ~/linux/linux-2.6.17.8/
```

The most common location for PCI IDs in the kernel source tree is *include/linux/pci_ids.h*. Search that file for our vendor product number:

```
$ grep -i 0x10ec include/linux/pci_ids.h
#define PCI_VENDOR_ID_REALTEK           0x10ec
```

---

* Some 64-bit processors will show the leading bus number for PCI devices in the output of *lspci*, but for the majority of the common Linux machines, it will not show up by default.

The defined value here, PCI_VENDOR_ID_REALTEK is what will probably be used in any kernel driver that purports to support devices from this manufacturer.

To be safe, also look in this file for our device ID, as it is also sometimes described there:

```
$ grep -i 0x8139 include/linux/pci_ids.h
#define PCI_DEVICE_ID_REALTEK_8139      0x8139
```

That definition will be useful later.

Now look for driver source files referring to this vendor definition:

```
$ grep -Rl PCI_VENDOR_ID_REALTEK *
include/linux/pci_ids.h
drivers/net/r8169.c
drivers/net/8139too.c
drivers/net/8139cp.c
```

We don't need to look at the first file listed here, *pci_ids.h*, because that is where we found the original definition. But the files *r8139.c*, *8139too.c*, and *8169cp.c* in the *drivers/net/* subdirectory should be examined more closely.

Open one of these files in an editor and search for PCI_VENDOR_ID_REALTEK. In the file *drivers/net/r8169.c*, it shows up in this section of code:

```
static struct pci_device_id rtl8169_pci_tbl[] = {
        { PCI_DEVICE(PCI_VENDOR_ID_REALTEK, 0x8169), },
        { PCI_DEVICE(PCI_VENDOR_ID_REALTEK, 0x8129), },
        { PCI_DEVICE(PCI_VENDOR_ID_DLINK,   0x4300), },
        { PCI_DEVICE(0x16ec,                0x0116), },
        { PCI_VENDOR_ID_LINKSYS,            0x1032, PCI_ANY_ID, 0x0024, },
        {0,},
};
```

All PCI drivers contain a list of the different devices that they support. That list is contained in a structure of struct pci_device_id values, just like this one. That is what we need to look at in order to determine whether our device is supported by this driver. The vendor value matches here, but the second value after the vendor is the device value. Our device has the value 0x8139, while this driver supports the device values of 0x8169 and 0x8129 for devices with the vendor ID of PCI_VENDOR_ID_REALTEK. So this driver will not support our device.

Moving on to the next file, *drivers/net/8139too.c*, we find the string PCI_VENDOR_ID_REALTEK in the following bit of code:

```
if (pdev->vendor == PCI_VENDOR_ID_REALTEK &&
    pdev->device == PCI_DEVICE_ID_REALTEK_8139 && pci_rev >= 0x20) {
    dev_info(&pdev->dev,
            "This (id %04x:%04x rev %02x) is an enhanced 8139C+ chip\n",
            pdev->vendor, pdev->device, pci_rev);
    dev_info(&pdev->dev,
            "Use the \"8139cp\" driver for improved performance and
stability.\n");
}
```

The use of the PCI_VENDOR_ID_REALTEK value here also corresponds with the code that checks whether the PCI device ID matches the PCI_DEVICE_ID_REALTEK_8139 value. If it does, the driver is to print out a message that says: "Use the 8139cp driver for improved performance and stability." Perhaps we should look at that driver next. Even if we did not have such a visible clue, the 8139too.c driver does not have the vendor and device ID pair that we are looking for in a struct pci_device_id variable, so that gives us the clue that it will not support our device.

Finally, look at the *drivers/net/8139cp.c* file. It uses the PCI_VENDOR_ID_REALTEK definition in the following code segment:

```
static struct pci_device_id cp_pci_tbl[] = {
        { PCI_VENDOR_ID_REALTEK, PCI_DEVICE_ID_REALTEK_8139,
          PCI_ANY_ID, PCI_ANY_ID, 0, 0, },
        { PCI_VENDOR_ID_TTTECH, PCI_DEVICE_ID_TTTECH_MC322,
          PCI_ANY_ID, PCI_ANY_ID, 0, 0, },
        { },
};
MODULE_DEVICE_TABLE(pci, cp_pci_tbl);
```

Here is a use of both our vendor and device ID values in a struct pci_device_id variable. This driver should support our device.

Now that we have the driver name, we can work backward, as shown in the first section in this chapter, to find the proper kernel configuration value that should be enabled to build this driver.

In summary, here are the steps needed in order to find which PCI driver can control a specific PCI device:

1. Find the PCI bus ID of the device for which you want to find the driver, using *lspci*.

2. Go into the */sys/bus/pci/devices/0000:bus_id* directory, where *bus_id* is the PCI bus ID found in the previous step.

3. Read the values of the vendor and device files in the PCI device directory.

4. Move back to the kernel source tree and look in *include/linux/pci_ids.h* for the PCI vendor and device IDs found in the previous step.

5. Search the kernel source tree for references to those values in drivers. Both the vendor and device ID should be in a struct pci_device_id definition.

6. Search the kernel Makefiles for the CONFIG_ rule that builds this driver by using *find* and *grep*:

   ```
   $ find -type f -name Makefile | xargs grep DRIVER_NAME
   ```

7. Search in the kernel configuration system for that configuration value and go to the location in the menu that it specifies to enable that driver to be built.

USB Devices

Finding the specific driver for a USB device is much like finding the driver for a PCI device as described in the previous section, with only minor differences in finding the bus ID values.

In this example, let's find the driver that is needed for a USB wireless device. As with the PCI device example, the details in this example will be different from your situation, but the steps involved should be relevant to any type of USB device for which you wish to find a working driver.

As with the PCI device, the bus ID must be found for the USB device you wish to find the driver for. To do this, you can use the *lsusb* program that comes in the *usbutils* package.

The *lsusb* program shows all USB devices attached to the system. As you do not know what the specific device you're looking for is called, start by looking at all devices:

```
$ /usr/sbin/lsusb
Bus 002 Device 003: ID 045e:0023 Microsoft Corp. Trackball Optical
Bus 002 Device 001: ID 0000:0000
Bus 005 Device 003: ID 0409:0058 NEC Corp. HighSpeed Hub
Bus 005 Device 001: ID 0000:0000
Bus 004 Device 003: ID 157e:300d
Bus 004 Device 002: ID 045e:001c Microsoft Corp.
Bus 004 Device 001: ID 0000:0000
Bus 003 Device 001: ID 0000:0000
Bus 001 Device 001: ID 0000:0000
```

The devices with an ID of 0000:0000 can be ignored, as they are USB host controllers that drive the bus itself. Filtering them away leaves us with four devices:

```
$ /usr/sbin/lsusb | grep -v 0000:0000
Bus 002 Device 003: ID 045e:0023 Microsoft Corp. Trackball Optical
Bus 005 Device 003: ID 0409:0058 NEC Corp. HighSpeed Hub
Bus 004 Device 003: ID 157e:300d
Bus 004 Device 002: ID 045e:001c Microsoft Corp.
```

Because USB devices are easy to remove, unplug the device you want to find the driver for and run *lsusb* again:

```
$ /usr/sbin/lsusb | grep -v 0000:0000
Bus 002 Device 003: ID 045e:0023 Microsoft Corp. Trackball Optical
Bus 005 Device 003: ID 0409:0058 NEC Corp. HighSpeed Hub
Bus 004 Device 002: ID 045e:001c Microsoft Corp.
```

The third device is now missing, which means the device shown as:

```
Bus 004 Device 003: ID 157e:300d
```

is the device you want to find the driver for.

If you replace the device and look at the output of *lsusb* again, the device number will have changed:

```
$ /usr/sbin/lsusb | grep 157e
Bus 004 Device 004: ID 157e:300d
```

This is because the USB device numbers are not unique, but change every time a device is plugged in. What is stable is the vendor and product ID, shown here by *lsusb* as two four-digit values with a : between them. For this device, the vendor ID is 157e and the product ID is 300d. Write down the values you find, as you will use them in future steps.

As with the PCI device, we will search the kernel source code for the USB vendor and product IDs in order to find the proper driver to control this device. Unfortunately, no single file contains all of the USB vendor IDs, as PCI has. So a search of the whole kernel source tree is necessary:

```
$ grep -i -R -l 157e drivers/*
drivers/atm/pca200e.data
drivers/atm/pca200e_ecd.data
drivers/atm/sba200e_ecd.data
drivers/net/wireless/zd1211rw/zd_usb.c
drivers/scsi/ql1040_fw.h
drivers/scsi/ql1280_fw.h
drivers/scsi/qlogicpti_asm.c
```

We know this is a USB wireless device, and not an ATM or SCSI device, so we can safely ignore the files found in the *atm* and *scsi* directories. That leaves the *drivers/net/wireless/zd1211rw/zd_usb.c* filename to investigate.

zd_usb.c shows the string 157e in the following chunk of code:

```
static struct usb_device_id usb_ids[] = {
        /* ZD1211 */
        { USB_DEVICE(0x0ace, 0x1211), .driver_info = DEVICE_ZD1211 },
        { USB_DEVICE(0x07b8, 0x6001), .driver_info = DEVICE_ZD1211 },
        { USB_DEVICE(0x126f, 0xa006), .driver_info = DEVICE_ZD1211 },
        { USB_DEVICE(0x6891, 0xa727), .driver_info = DEVICE_ZD1211 },
        { USB_DEVICE(0x0df6, 0x9071), .driver_info = DEVICE_ZD1211 },
        { USB_DEVICE(0x157e, 0x300b), .driver_info = DEVICE_ZD1211 },
        /* ZD1211B */
        { USB_DEVICE(0x0ace, 0x1215), .driver_info = DEVICE_ZD1211B },
        { USB_DEVICE(0x157e, 0x300d), .driver_info = DEVICE_ZD1211B },
        {}
};
```

Like PCI drivers, USB drivers tell the kernel what devices they support in order for the kernel to bind the driver to the device. This is done by using a struct usb_device_id variable, as shown here. This is a list of the different vendor and product IDs that are supported by this driver. The line:

```
{ USB_DEVICE(0x157e, 0x300b), .driver_info = DEVICE_ZD1211 },
```

shows that our vendor and product IDs are supported by this driver.

Once you have the driver name that is necessary to control this device, work backward through the kernel *Makefiles*, as described earlier in the chapter, to determine how to enable this driver to be built properly.

In summary, the steps needed in order to find which USB driver will control a specific USB device are:

1. Find the USB vendor and product ID of device for which you want to find the driver, using *lsusb* after adding and then removing the device to see what changes in the list.

2. Search the kernel source tree for the vendor and product ID of the USB device. Both the vendor and product ID should be in a struct usb_device_id definition.

3. Search the kernel Makefiles for the `CONFIG_` rule that builds this driver by using *find* and *grep*:

```
$ find -type f -name Makefile | xargs grep DRIVER_NAME
```

4. Search in the kernel configuration system for that configuration value and go to the location in the menu that it specifies to enable that driver to be built.

Root Filesystem

The root filesystem is the filesystem from which the main portion of the running system boots. It contains all of the initial programs that start up the distro, and also usually contains the entire system configuration for the machine. In short, it is very important, and must be able to be found by the kernel at boot time in order for things to work properly.

If your newly configured kernel dies at boot time with an error such as:

```
VFS: Cannot open root device hda2 (03:02)
Please append a correct "root=" boot option
Kernal panic: VFS: Unable to mount root fs on 03:02
```

then the root filesystem wasn't found. If you are not using a ramdisk image at boot time, it is usually recommended that you build both the filesystem that you use for your root partition, and the disk controller for that disk, into the kernel, instead of having it as a module. If you use a ramdisk at boot time, you should be safe building these portions as modules.

 How can you determine whether you are using a ramdisk at boot time? In Chapter 5 we mention using the distribution installation script to install the kernel versus doing the installation on your own. If you are using the distribution installation script, you are probably using a ramdisk. If you are installing it on your own, you are probably not.

The following subsections show how to let the kernel find the root filesystem during boot.

Filesystem type

First, the type of filesystem that the root partition is using needs to be determined. To do that, look in the output of the *mount* command:

```
$ mount | grep " / "
/dev/sda2 on / type ext3 (rw,noatime)
```

We are interested in the type of the filesystem, which is shown after the word type. In this example, it is ext3. This is the type of filesystem that the root partition is using. Go into the kernel configuration system and make sure that this filesystem type is enabled, as described in Chapter 8.

Disk controller

In the output of the *mount* command shown earlier, the first portion of the line shows which block device the root filesystem is mounted on. In this example, it's */dev/sda2*. Now that the filesystem is configured properly in your kernel, you must also make sure that this block device will also work correctly. To find out which drivers are needed for this, you need to look at *sysfs* again.

All block devices show up in *sysfs* in either */sys/block* or in */sys/class/block*, depending on the version of the kernel you are using. In either location, the block devices are a tree, with the different partitions being children of the main device:

```
$ tree -d /sys/block/ | egrep "hd|sd"
|-- hdc
|-- hdd
`-- sda
    |-- sda1
    |-- sda2
    |-- sda3
```

Given the information in the *mount* command, you need to ensure that the sda2 device is configured properly. Because this is a partition (disk partitions are numbered, while main block devices are not), the whole sda device must be configured. (Without the main block device, there is no way to access the individual partitions on that device.)

The sda block device is represented just like the network device we looked at earlier in this chapter. There is a symlink in the device's directory called device that points to the logical device that controls this block device:

```
$ ls -l /sys/block/sda
...
device -> ../../devices/pci0000:00/0000:00:1f.2/host0/target0:0:0/0:0:0:0
...
```

Now you need to start walking up the chain of devices in *sysfs* to find out which driver is controlling this device:

```
$ ls -l /sys/devices/pci0000:00/0000:00:1f.2/host0/target0:0:0/0:0:0:0
...
driver -> ../../../../../../bus/scsi/drivers/sd
...
```

Here we see that the SCSI disk controller driver is responsible for making this device work. So we know we need to configure SCSI disk support into our kernel configuration.

Continuing up the directory chain in *sysfs*, try to find where the driver is that controls the hardware:

```
$ ls -l /sys/devices/pci0000:00/0000:00:1f.2/host0/target0:0:0
...
```

There is no link called driver in this directory, so go back up one more level:

```
$ ls -l /sys/devices/pci0000:00/0000:00:1f.2/host0
...
```

Again, no driver here. Continuing on up one more level:

```
$ ls -l /sys/devices/pci0000:00/0000:00:1f.2
    ...
driver -> ../../../bus/pci/drivers/ata_piix
    ...
```

There! This is the disk controller we need to ensure is in our kernel configuration.

So for this root filesystem, we need to enable the ext3, sd, and ata_piix drivers in our kernel configuration so that we will be able to successfully boot our kernel on this hardware.

Helper Script

As mentioned near the beginning of this chapter, files and directories within *sysfs* change from one release of the kernel to another. Here is a script that is handy in determining the needed kernel driver and module module name for any device node in the system. It has been developed with the kernel developers responsible for *sysfs* and should successfully work on all future versions of the 2.6 kernel.

For instance, it makes short work of the previous example, when you had to get all of the proper drivers for the sda block device:

```
$ get-driver.sh sda
looking at sysfs device: /sys/devices/pci0000:00/0000:00:1f.2/host0/
target0:0:0/0:0:0:0
found driver: sd
found driver: ata_piix
```

I can also find all of the proper drivers needed for complex things such as USB-to-serial devices:

```
$ get-driver.sh ttyUSB0
looking at sysfs device: /sys/devices/pci0000:00/0000:00:1d.3/usb4/4-2/4-2.
3/4-2.3:1.0/ttyUSB0
found driver: pl2303 from module: pl2303
found driver: pl2303 from module: pl2303
found driver: usb from module: usbcore
found driver: usb from module: usbcore
found driver: usb from module: usbcore
found driver: uhci_hcd from module: uhci_hcd
```

You can download an example file containing this script from the book's web site, provided in the "How to Contact Us" section of the Preface.

The script follows:

```
#!/bin/sh
#
# Find all modules and drivers for a given class device.
#
if [ $# != "1" ] ; then
    echo
    echo "Script to display the drivers and modules for a specified sysfs
class device"
    echo "usage: $0 <CLASS_NAME>"
    echo
    echo "example usage:"
```

```
        echo "       $0 sda"
        echo "Will show all drivers and modules for the sda block device."
        echo
        exit 1
fi
DEV=$1
if test -e "$1"; then
    DEVPATH=$1
else
    # find sysfs device directory for device
    DEVPATH=$(find /sys/class -name "$1" | head -1)
    test -z "$DEVPATH" && DEVPATH=$(find /sys/block -name "$1" | head -1)
    test -z "$DEVPATH" && DEVPATH=$(find /sys/bus -name "$1" | head -1)
    if ! test -e "$DEVPATH"; then
        echo "no device found"
        exit 1
    fi
fi
echo "looking at sysfs device: $DEVPATH"
if test -L "$DEVPATH"; then
    # resolve class device link to device directory
    DEVPATH=$(readlink -f $DEVPATH)
    echo "resolve link to: $DEVPATH"
fi
if test -d "$DEVPATH"; then
    # resolve old-style "device" link to the parent device
    PARENT="$DEVPATH";
    while test "$PARENT" != "/"; do
        if test -L "$PARENT/device"; then
            DEVPATH=$(readlink -f $PARENT/device)
            echo "follow 'device' link to parent: $DEVPATH"
            break
        fi
        PARENT=$(dirname $PARENT)
    done
fi
while test "$DEVPATH" != "/"; do
    DRIVERPATH=
    DRIVER=
    MODULEPATH=
    MODULE=
    if test -e $DEVPATH/driver; then
        DRIVERPATH=$(readlink -f $DEVPATH/driver)
        DRIVER=$(basename $DRIVERPATH)
        echo -n "found driver: $DRIVER"
        if test -e $DRIVERPATH/module; then
            MODULEPATH=$(readlink -f $DRIVERPATH/module)
            MODULE=$(basename $MODULEPATH)
            echo -n " from module: $MODULE"
        fi
        echo
    fi
    DEVPATH=$(dirname $DEVPATH)
done
```

8

Kernel Configuration Recipes

Previous chapters taught the mechanics of reconfiguring the kernel; the payoff comes in this chapter where you can find all the most common kinds of changes people need to make to their kernels, with specific instructions on how to do so.

Disks

The Linux kernel supports a wide range of different disk types. This section shows how to configure the kernel so that it supports most of the more common types of disk controllers.

USB Storage

To use a USB storage device (commonly referred to as USB "flash" device, or an external USB disk drive) USB support must be first working properly. Refer to the recipe in the section called "USB" for how to do this.

A USB storage device can be identified by using the *lsusb* program. If the following command sequence produces the results shown, a USB storage device is present on the system:

```
$ /usr/sbin/lsusb -v | grep Storage
        bInterfaceClass         8 Mass Storage
```

Enable it as follows.

1. A USB Storage device is in reality a USB SCSI device that talks over a USB connection. Because of this, the SCSI subsystem must be enabled:

```
Device Drivers
    SCSI Device Support
        [*] SCSI Device Support
```

2. Also in the SCSI system, the "SCSI disk support" must be enabled in order for the device to be mounted properly:

```
Device Drivers
    SCSI Device Support
        [*] SCSI disk support
```

3. Enable USB Storage support:

```
Device Drivers
    USB Support
    [M] USB Mass Storage support
```

A number of specific USB storage devices are listed as separate configuration items, as they do not follow the standard USB specification and require special code. If you have one of these devices, please enable support for them.

IDE Disks

IDE disks are the most common type of PC disks. The device that enables them to work properly is an IDE disk controller. To determine whether you have a IDE disk controller on the system, use the *lspci* command in the following manner:*

```
$ /usr/sbin/lspci | grep IDE
00:1f.1 IDE interface: Intel Corporation 82801EB/ER (ICH5/ICH5R) IDE
Controller (rev 02)
00:1f.2 IDE interface: Intel Corporation 82801EB (ICH5) SATA Controller (rev
02)
```

Note that your response will probably not be identical; what is important is that the command shows some an IDE controller (the first device in the previous example.) If you find only SATA controllers, please see the next section "Serial ATA (SATA)." Now perform the following steps.

1. Enable PCI support for the kernel:

```
Bus options (PCI, PCMCIA, EISA, MCA, ISA)
    [*] PCI Support
```

2. Enable the IDE subsystem, and IDE support:

```
Device Drivers
    [*] ATA/ATAPI/MFM/RLL support
    [*]    Enhanced IDE/MFM/RLL disk/cdrom/tape/floppy support
```

3. In the ATA system, the specific type of IDE controller that you have must be enabled in order for it to work properly. To provide a good backup in case you choose the wrong type, select the "generic" IDE controller:

```
Device Drivers
    ATA/ATAPI/MFM/RLL support
        [*]      generic/default IDE chipset support
```

---

* Almost all distributions place the *lspci* program in the */usr/sbin/* directory, but some place it in other locations. To find out where it is located, enter:

```
$ which lspci
/usr/sbin/lspci
```

If you are using a distribution that puts it somewhere else, please use that path for whenever we discuss using *lspci*.

4. Enable the different PCI IDE controllers:

```
Device Drivers
    ATA/ATAPI/MFM/RLL support
        [*]     PCI IDE chipset support
```

This opens up a lengthy submenu of the different IDE controller types. Select the proper one based on the name of the device you found in the *lspci* step.

Serial ATA (SATA)

SATA is a type of disk controller that is the successor to the IDE disk controller. To determine if you have a SATA disk controller on the system, run the following command:

```
$ /usr/sbin/lspci | grep SATA
00:1f.2 IDE interface: Intel Corporation 82801EB (ICH5) SATA Controller (rev 02)
```

Note that your response will probably not be identical; what is important is that the command shows some SATA devices.

SATA disks use a kernel library called *libata* that handles most of the SATA-specific functionality. That library uses the SCSI layer to talk to the block layer, so several different kernel options need to be enabled in order for SATA disks to work properly.

1. Enable PCI support for the kernel:

```
Bus options (PCI, PCMCIA, EISA, MCA, ISA)
    [*] PCI Support
```

2. Enable the SCSI subsystem:

```
Device Drivers
    SCSI Device Support
        [*] SCSI Device Support
```

3. Also in the SCSI system, the SCSI disk support option must be enabled in order for the device to be mounted properly:

```
Device Drivers
    SCSI Device Support
        [*] SCSI disk support
```

4. The SATA options are under the "SCSI low-level drivers" section:

```
Device Drivers
    SCSI Device Support
        SCSI low-level drivers
            [*] Serial ATA (SATA) support
```

5. In that section, enable the specific SATA controller type that you have. Look at the output of the previously mentioned *lspci* command for a list of the types of SATA controllers that are present on your system. For example, most motherboards from Intel require the PIIX/ICH SATA driver (as the previous example showed):

```
Device Drivers
    SCSI Device Support
        SCSI low-level drivers
```

```
[*] Serial ATA (SATA) support
[*]    Intel PIIX/ICH SATA support
```

Burning a CD-ROM

Burning a CD-ROM is very simple on Linux. If your kernel can support reading from a CD-ROM, it can also support burning a CD-ROM. There are two ways to enable CD-ROM support in Linux, one for IDE drives and one for SCSI and SATA drives.

IDE CD-ROM drives

IDE CD-ROM drives are controlled by the same IDE controller as your main IDE disk drives. Make sure the IDE controller is properly supported as described earlier in "IDE Disks." If it is properly supported, only one other configuration item needs to be selected:

```
Device Drivers
    [*] ATA/ATAPI/MFM/RLL support
    [*]    Enhanced IDE/MFM/RLL disk/cdrom/tape/floppy support
    [M]       Include IDE/ATAPI CDROM support
```

SCSI and SATA CD-ROM drives

SATA and SCSI CD-ROM drives are controlled by the same controller as your main disk drives. Make sure the SATA or SCSI controller is properly supported. For SATA disks, see the earlier section "Serial ATA (SATA)."

To support SATA or SCSI CD-ROM drives, the SCSI CD-ROM driver must be enabled:

```
Device Drivers
    SCSI Device Support
        [*] SCSI CDROM support
```

Once that is enabled, the SATA or SCSI CD-ROM drive should work properly.

Devices

Linux supports a vast range of different types of devices (more than any other operating system ever has). This section shows how to enable some of the more common types.

USB

Linux supports many different types of USB devices. To enable USB support, you must first enable support for a USB controller, which drives the USB connection on the machine.

To determine if your machine has a USB controller, and which type it is, run the following command:

```
$ /usr/sbin/lspci | grep USB
00:1d.0 USB Controller: Intel Corporation 82801EB/ER (ICH5/ICH5R) USB UHCI
Controller #1 (rev 02)
00:1d.1 USB Controller: Intel Corporation 82801EB/ER (ICH5/ICH5R) USB UHCI
Controller #2 (rev 02)
00:1d.2 USB Controller: Intel Corporation 82801EB/ER (ICH5/ICH5R) USB UHCI
Controller #3 (rev 02)
00:1d.3 USB Controller: Intel Corporation 82801EB/ER (ICH5/ICH5R) USB UHCI
Controller #4 (rev 02)
00:1d.7 USB Controller: Intel Corporation 82801EB/ER (ICH5/ICH5R) USB2 EHCI
Controller (rev 02)
```

Note that your response will probably not be identical; what is important is that the command shows some USB controllers.

1. Enable PCI support for the kernel:

```
Bus options (PCI, PCMCIA, EISA, MCA, ISA)
    [*] PCI Support
```

2. Enable USB support for the kernel:

```
Device Drivers
    USB Support
        [M] Support for Host-side USB
```

3. Enable the specific USB Host controllers for your machine (it is safe to enable them all if you do not know which you have):

```
Device Drivers
    USB Support
    ---     USB Host Controller Drivers
    [M]     EHCI HCD (USB 2.0) support
    [M]     OHCI HCD support
    [M]     UHCI HCD (most Intel and VIA) support
```

4. Individual USB devices also need their drivers to be enabled. A large majority of them are under the main USB driver section:

```
Device Drivers
    USB Support
```

But some devices, such as USB video and DVB and sound, are listed in the section controlling all of these types of devices. For example, the USB sound driver can be found under the Sound menu:

```
Device drivers
    Sound
        [*] Sound card support
            [*] Advanced Linux Sound Architecture
                USB Devices
                    [M] USB Audio/MIDI driver
```

If you want to insert USB storage devices (USB flash), look now at the section called "USB Storage," at the beginning of this chapter.

IEEE 1394 (FireWire)

IEEE 1394 is commonly known by the name FireWire, the name by which Apple Computer publicized it. IEEE 1394 is a high-speed bus that connects external devices, much as USB does.

To determine whether your machine has a FireWire controller and which type it is, run the following command:

```
$ /usr/sbin/lspci | grep FireWire
06:0c.0 FireWire (IEEE 1394): Texas Instruments TSB43AB22/A IEEE-1394a-2000
Controller (PHY/Link)
06:0d.2 FireWire (IEEE 1394): Creative Labs SB Audigy FireWire Port (rev 04)
```

Note that your response will probably not be identical; what is important is that the command shows some FireWire controllers.

1. Enable PCI support for the kernel:

```
Bus options (PCI, PCMCIA, EISA, MCA, ISA)
    [*] PCI Support
```

2. Enable IEEE 1394 support for the kernel:

```
Device Drivers
    IEEE 1394 (FireWire) support
        [*] IEEE 1394 (FireWire) support
```

3. Enable the specific type of FireWire host controller you have:

```
Device Drivers
    IEEE 1394 (FireWire) support
        [*] IEEE 1394 (FireWire) support
        ---     Device Drivers
        [M]     Texas Instruments PCILynx support
        [M]     OHCI-1394 support
```

4. Finally, enable the specific type of FireWire devices you have:

```
Device Drivers
    IEEE 1394 (FireWire) support
        [*] IEEE 1394 (FireWire) support
        ---     Protocol Drivers
        [M]     OHCI-1394 Video support
        [M]     SBP-2 support (Harddisks etc.)
        [ ]       Enable Phys DMA support for SBP2 (Debug)
        [M]     Ethernet over 1394
        [M]     OHCI-DV I/O support
        [M]     Raw IEEE1394 I/O support
```

PCI Hotplug

PCI hotplug systems are becoming more popular with the use of ExpressCard and laptop docking stations.

To determine whether your machine has an ExpressCard controller, look at the hardware to see whether an ExpressCard card can be plugged into it.

1. Enable PCI support for the kernel:

```
Bus options (PCI, PCMCIA, EISA, MCA, ISA)
    [*] PCI Support
```

2. Enable PCI hotplug support for the kernel:

```
Bus options (PCI, PCMCIA, EISA, MCA, ISA)
    [*] PCI Support
    PCI Hotplug Support
        [M] Support for PCI Hotplug (EXPERIMENTAL)
```

3. There is a wide range of different types of PCI hotplug controllers. For most laptops and for ExpressCard support, enable the ACPI controller:

```
Bus options (PCI, PCMCIA, EISA, MCA, ISA)
    [*] PCI Support
    PCI Hotplug Support
        [M] Support for PCI Hotplug (EXPERIMENTAL)
        [M]   ACPI PCI Hotplug driver
```

4. Also enable the PCI Express controller:

```
Bus options (PCI, PCMCIA, EISA, MCA, ISA)
    [*] PCI Support
    [*] PCI Express Support
    [M]   PCI Express Hotplug driver
```

PCMCIA/CardBus

PCMCIA and CardBus device support is in almost every laptop manufactured. Newer laptops, however, are switching to the ExpressCard format (see the PCI Hotplug recipe in the previous section, "PCI Hotplug").

To determine whether your machine has a PCMCIA controller, look at the hardware to see whether a PCMCIA card can be plugged into it.

1. Enable PCI support for the kernel:

```
Bus options (PCI, PCMCIA, EISA, MCA, ISA)
    [*] PCI Support
```

2. Enable PCCARD support for the kernel:

```
Bus options (PCI, PCMCIA, EISA, MCA, ISA)
    PCCARD (PCMCIA/CardBus) support
        [M] PCCard (PCMCIA/CardBus) support
```

3. Enable both PCMCIA and CardBus support to cover the widest range of devices:

```
Bus options (PCI, PCMCIA, EISA, MCA, ISA)
    PCCARD (PCMCIA/CardBus) support
        [M] PCCard (PCMCIA/CardBus) support
        [M]   16-bit PCMCIA support
        [*]   32-bit CardBus support
```

Enable the card bridge type for your laptop. The most common one is the "yenta-like" controller:

```
Bus options (PCI, PCMCIA, EISA, MCA, ISA)
    PCCARD (PCMCIA/CardBus) support
        [M] PCCard (PCMCIA/CardBus) support
```

```
[M]    CardBus yenta-compatible bridge support
[ ]    Cirrus PD6729 compatible bridge support
[ ]    i82092 compatible bridge support
[ ]    i82365 compatible bridge support
[ ]    Databook TCIC host bridge support
```

Sound (ALSA)

Advanced Linux Sound Architecture (ALSA) is the current sound system for the Linux kernel. An earlier sound system (OSS) has been deprecated, and almost all of the older drivers have been removed from the kernel source tree.

To determine which type of sound controller is present in your machine, and what type it is, run the following command:

```
$ /usr/sbin/lspci | grep -i audio
00:1f.5 Multimedia audio controller: Intel Corporation 82801EB/ER (ICH5/
ICH5R) AC'97 Audio Controller (rev 02)
06:0d.0 Multimedia audio controller: Creative Labs SB Audigy (rev 04)
```

Note that your response will probably not be identical; what is important is that the command shows some Audio controllers.

1. Enable basic sound support:

   ```
   Device Drivers
       Sound
           [M] Sound Card Support
   ```

2. Enable ALSA:

   ```
   Device Drivers
       Sound
           [M] Sound Card Support
           [M] Advanced Linux Sound Architecture
   ```

3. There are a number of different base ALSA options, such as support for the older OSS sound protocol. If you have older applications, you should enable the related options:

   ```
   Device Drivers
       Sound
           [M] Sound Card Support
               [M] Advanced Linux Sound Architecture
               [M]    OSS Mixer API
               [M]    OSS PCM (digital audio) API
               [ ]        OSS PCM (digital audio) API - Include plugin system
   ```

4. Enable the specific type of sound device that you have. PCI sound cards are under the PCI submenu:

   ```
   Device Drivers
       Sound
           [M] Sound Card Support
               [M] Advanced Linux Sound Architecture
                   PCI Devices
   ```

CPU

If you wish to have the Linux kernel run as fast as possible for your specific processor and hardware type, there are a few options that you can set to get the last bit of performance out of the hardware. This section will show some of the different processor-specific options that you can tune for your processor.

Processor Types

A wide range of specific processor options are available to be changed in the Linux kernel. The most important one for our purpose specifies the exact type of CPU you are using this kernel for. To determine the type of processor you are using, run the following command:

```
$ cat /proc/cpuinfo | grep "model name"
model name      : Intel(R) Xeon(TM) CPU 3.20GHz
```

Note that your response will probably not be identical; what is important is that the command shows the model name of the processor present on the system.

1. Select the subarchitecture type of the processor:

```
Processor type and features
    Subarchitecture Type
        (X) PC-compatible
        ( ) AMD Elan
        ( ) Voyager (NCR)
        ( ) NUMAQ (IBM/Sequent)
        ( ) Summit/EXA (IBM x440)
        ( ) Support for other sub-arch SMP systems with more than 8 CPUs
        ( ) SGI 320/540 (Visual Workstation)
        ( ) Generic architecture (Summit, bigsmp, ES7000, default)
        ( ) Support for Unisys ES7000 IA32 series
```

Only if your machine is one of the other types in the preceding list should you select anything other than the PC-compatible option. However, if you wish to create a single kernel that will run on all of the types of machines shown, select the Generic architecture option. Some of the above options might not be present if you have not also selected the Symmetric multi-processing support option.

2. Select the processor family type. The PC-compatible option needs to be selected from the previous options for this submenu to be displayed:

```
Processor type and features
    Processor family
        ( ) 386
        ( ) 486
        ( ) 586/K5/5x86/6x86/6x86MX
        ( ) Pentium-Classic
        ( ) Pentium-MMX
        ( ) Pentium-Pro
        ( ) Pentium-II/Celeron(pre-Coppermine)
        ( ) Pentium-III/Celeron(Coppermine)/Pentium-III Xeon
        ( ) Pentium M
        (X) Pentium-4/Celeron(P4-based)/Pentium-4 M/Xeon
```

```
( ) K6/K6-II/K6-III
( ) Athlon/Duron/K7
( ) Opteron/Athlon64/Hammer/K8
( ) Crusoe
( ) Efficeon
( ) Winchip-C6
( ) Winchip-2
( ) Winchip-2A/Winchip-3
( ) GeodeGX1
( ) Geode GX/LX
( ) CyrixIII/VIA-C3
( ) VIA C3-2 (Nehemiah)
( ) Generic x86 support
```

For more details on this configuration item, please refer to the entry for M386 in Chapter 11 for a full description of how to pick the proper processor type depending on what processor you have, and what range of machines you wish the kernel to run on.

SMP

If your system contains more than one CPU, or a Hyperthreaded or Dual Core CPU, you should select the multiprocessor option for the Linux kernel in order to take advantage of the additional processors. Unless you do, you will be wasting the other processors by not using them at all.

Enable multiprocessing:

```
Processor type and features
    [*] Symmetric multi-processing support
```

Preemption

Systems running as servers have very different workload requirements from those being used as a desktop for video and audio applications. The kernel allows different modes of "preemption" in order to handle these different workloads. *Preemption* is the ability of the kernel to interrupt itself while it is doing something else, in order to work on something with a higher priority, such as updating a sound or video program.

To change to a different preemption model, use this menu:

```
Processor type and features
    Preemption Model
        (X) No Forced Preemption (Server)
    ( ) Voluntary Kernel Preemption (Desktop)
    ( ) Preemptible Kernel (Low-Latency Desktop)
```

If you wish to make the kernel even more responsive to higher priority tasks than the general preemption option provides, you can also allow interruptions to one of the main internal kernel locks:

```
Processor type and features
    [*] Preempt The Big Kernel Lock
```

This option is able to be selected only if you have already selected either the `Preemptible Kernel` or `Symmetric multi-processing support` options.

Suspend

The Linux kernel has the ability to suspend itself to disk, allowing you to disconnect the power, and then at a later time, power up and resume exactly where the machine was when it was suspended. This functionality is very useful on laptops that run Linux.

Enable this by selecting:

```
Power management options (ACPI, APM)
    [*] Software Suspend
```

The kernel needs to know where to save the suspended kernel image to, and then later where to resume it from. This location is usually a kernel swap partition on the disk. To specify which partition this should be set:

```
Power management options (ACPI, APM)
    (/dev/hda3) Default resume partition
```

Make sure you specify the proper partition to suspend the machine to, and do not use a partition that is being used by the system for data. The proper partition name can be found by running the following command:

```
$ /sbin/swapon -s | grep dev | cut -f 1 -d ' '
/dev/hda3
```

Use the output of the preceding command in this kernel configuration option, and on the kernel boot line where it specifies where the kernel should be resumed from. After the machine has been suspended, to have it resume properly, pass the `resume=/dev/swappartition` argument to the kernel command line to have it use the proper image. If you do not want to have the suspended image restored, use the `noresume` kernel command-line argument.

CPU Frequency Scaling

Most modern processors can slow down the internal clock of the processor to conserve power and battery life. Linux supports this ability and offers a variety of power "governors." Different governors implement different heuristics in order to determine how to vary the processor speed depending on the system load and other variables.

1. Enable the basic frequency scaling functionality:

```
Power management options (ACPI, APM)
    [*] CPU Frequency scaling
```

2. Select the different type of frequency governors you wish to use:

```
Power management options (ACPI, APM)
    [*] CPU Frequency scaling
    [*]     'performance' governor
    [*]     'powersave' governor
    [*]     'userspace' governor for userspace frequency scaling
    [*]     'ondemand' cpufreq policy governor
    [*]     'conservative' cpufreq governor
```

For more information on what the different governors do, see the entry for CPU_FREQ in Chapter 11.

3. Select the default governor you wish to have running when the machine boots:

```
Power management options (ACPI, APM)
    [*] CPU Frequency scaling
            Default CPUFreq governor (performance)
```

4. Select the specific processor type on the machine. For details on how to determine the processor type of the machine, see the earlier section, "Processor Types."

```
Power management options (ACPI, APM)
    [*] CPU Frequency scaling
    ---     CPUFreq processor drivers
    [ ]     ACPI Processor P-States driver
    [ ]     AMD Mobile K6-2/K6-3 PowerNow!
    [ ]     AMD Mobile Athlon/Duron PowerNow!
    [ ]     AMD Opteron/Athlon64 PowerNow!
    [ ]     Cyrix MediaGX/NatSemi Geode Suspend Modulation
    [*]     Intel Enhanced SpeedStep
    [*]        Use ACPI tables to decode valid frequency/voltage pairs
    [*]        Built-in tables for Banias CPUs
    [ ]     Intel Speedstep on ICH-M chipsets (ioport interface)
    [ ]     Intel SpeedStep on 440BX/ZX/MX chipsets (SMI interface)
    [ ]     Intel Pentium 4 clock modulation
    [ ]     nVidia nForce2 FSB changing
    [ ]     Transmeta LongRun
```

Different Memory Models

Linux on 32-bit Intel hardware can access up to 64 GB of memory, but the address space of the 32-bit processor is only 4 GB. To work around this limitation, Linux can map the additional memory into another area and then switch to it when other tasks need it. But if your machine has a smaller amount of memory, it is easier for Linux not to have to worry about handling the bigger areas, so it is beneficial to tell the kernel how much memory you want it to support. For a more detailed description of this option, please see the entry for HIGHMEM in Chapter 11.

Linux supports three different memory models for 32-bit Intel processors, depending on the memory available:

- Under 1 GB of physical memory
- Between 1 and 4 GB of physical memory
- Greater than 4 GB of physical memory

To select the amount of memory:

```
Processor type and features
    High Memory Support
        (X) off
        ( ) 4GB
        ( ) 64GB
```

ACPI

On almost all modern Intel-based systems, ACPI is required in order for the machine to work properly. ACPI is a standard that allows the BIOS of the computer to work with the operating system in order to access the hardware in an indirect manner, in the hope of handling a wide range of devices with relatively little code specific to each operating system. ACPI also provides a facility to help suspend and resume a machine and control the speed of the processor and fans. If you have a laptop, it is recommended that you enable this option.

To enable ACPI:

```
Power management options (ACPI, APM)
    ACPI (Advanced Configuration and Power Interface) Support
        [*] ACPI Support
```

There are a wide range of different ACPI "drivers" that control different types of ACPI devices. You should enable the specific ones that you have on your machine:

```
Power management options (ACPI, APM)
    ACPI (Advanced Configuration and Power Interface) Support
        [*] ACPI Support
        [*]    AC Adapter
        [*]    Battery
        [*]    Button
        [*]    Video
        [*]    Generic Hotkey (EXPERIMENTAL)
        [*]    Fan
        [*]    Processor
        [*]      Thermal Zone
        [ ]    ASUS/Medion Laptop Extras
        [ ]    IBM ThinkPad Laptop Extras
        [ ]    Toshiba Laptop Extras
```

Networking

Networking is required for almost all machines today, and Linux supports almost every networking option available. Here I am going to show only a few of the wide variety that are present.

For all networking options, including different drivers, the main network configuration option must be enabled:

```
Networking
    [*] Networking support
```

The TCP/IP option should also be selected so that the machine can talk to other machines on the Internet:

```
Networking
    [*] Networking support
            Networking options
                [*] TCP/IP networking
```

Netfilter

The Netfilter portion of the Linux kernel is a framework for filtering and manipulating all network packets that pass through the machine. It is commonly used if you wish to enable a firewall on the machine to protect it from different systems on the Internet, or to use the machine as a proxy for other machines on the network. For more details on what Netfilter is good for, please see the entry for NETFILTER in Chapter 11.

1. To enable the main Netfilter option:

```
Networking
    [*] Networking support
        Networking options
            [*] Network packet filtering (replaces ipchains)
```

2. It is recommended that you enable the Netfilter netlink interface and Xtables support when using netlink:

```
Networking
    [*] Networking support
        Networking options
            [*] Network packet filtering (replaces ipchains)
                Core Netfilter Configuration
                    [*] Netfilter netlink interface
                    [*] Netfilter Xtables support (required for ip_
                        tables)
```

3. The different protocols that you wish to filter should also be selected:

```
Networking
    [*] Networking support
        Networking options
            [*] Network packet filtering (replaces ipchains)
                IP: Netfilter Configuration
                    [M] Connection tracking (required for masq/NAT)
                    [ ]     Connection tracking flow accounting
                    [ ]     Connection mark tracking support
                    [ ]     Connection tracking events (EXPERIMENTAL)
                    [ ]     SCTP protocol connection tracking support
                            (EXPERIMENTAL)
                    [M]     FTP protocol support
                    [ ]     IRC protocol support
                    [ ]     NetBIOS name service protocol support
                            (EXPERIMENTAL)
                    [M]     TFTP protocol support
                    [ ]     Amanda backup protocol support
                    [ ]     PPTP protocol support
                    [ ]     H.323 protocol support (EXPERIMENTAL)
```

Network Drivers

Linux supports a wide array of different network devices. The most common one is a PCI network device, into which an Ethernet cable can be plugged. To determine whether you have a PCI network device on the system, and what type it is, run the following command:

```
$ /usr/sbin/lspci | grep Ethernet
03:0c.0 Ethernet controller: D-Link System Inc RTL8139 Ethernet (rev 10)
03:0e.0 Ethernet controller: Intel Corporation 82545GM Gigabit Ethernet
Controller (rev 04)
```

Note that your response will probably not be identical; what is important is that the command shows some PCI Ethernet devices.

1. Enable PCI support for the kernel:

```
Bus options (PCI, PCMCIA, EISA, MCA, ISA)
[*] PCI Support
```

2. Enable basic network device support:

```
Device Drivers
    Network device support
        [*] Network device support
```

3. Then comes the fun task of finding the specific device drivers for your hardware. The most common place to find Ethernet devices for modern hardware is in the gigabit section of the driver selection:

```
Device Drivers
    Network device support
        [*] Network device support
            Ethernet (1000 Mbit)
```

Some older ethernet devices will be found in the 10- and 100-Mbit section:

```
Device Drivers
    Network device support
        [*] Network device support
            Ethernet (10 or 100Mbit)
```

Look through those sections to find the proper driver for your specific devices.

IrDA

IrDA is an infrared protocol used by a number of laptops and PDAs to communicate over very short distances. It is prevalent on older hardware, with newer hardware using Bluetooth to communicate instead. See the later section, "Bluetooth," for configuring Bluetooth.

1. IrDA is a network protocol, so it can be found under the networking main menu:

```
Networking
    [*] Networking support
    [*]    IrDA (infrared) subsystem support
```

2. A number of different IrDA protocols can be selected, depending on the type of device you wish to communicate with and the program used to do the communication:

```
Networking
    [*] Networking support
        --- IrDA (infrared) subsystem support
        ---     IrDA protocols
        [*]     IrLAN protocol (NEW)
```

```
[*]    IrCOMM protocol (NEW)
[*]    Ultra (connectionless) protocol (NEW)
```

3. There are a wide range of different types of IrDA devices, some serial, some PCI, and others based on USB. To select the specific type of IrDA device you have, choose it under the driver submenu for IrDA:

```
Networking
   [*] Networking support
      --- IrDA (infrared) subsystem support
          Infrared-port device drivers
          --- SIR device drivers
          [ ] IrTTY (uses Linux serial driver)
          --- Dongle support
          --- Old SIR device drivers
          --- Old Serial dongle support
          --- FIR device drivers
          [ ] IrDA USB dongles
          [ ] SigmaTel STIr4200 bridge (EXPERIMENTAL)
          [ ] NSC PC87108/PC87338
          [ ] Winbond W83977AF (IR)
          [ ] Toshiba Type-O IR Port
          [ ] SMSC IrCC (EXPERIMENTAL)
          [ ] ALi M5123 FIR (EXPERIMENTAL)
          [ ] VLSI 82C147 SIR/MIR/FIR (EXPERIMENTAL)
          [ ] VIA VT8231/VT1211 SIR/MIR/FIR
```

Bluetooth

Bluetooth is a wireless technology that was created to replace IrDA to talk between devices over a very short distance. It is a short-range wireless technology that was designed as a replacement for cables, operates within a 10 meter radius, and is commonly used in mobile phones.

1. Bluetooth is a network protocol, so it can be found under the networking main menu:

```
Networking
   [*] Networking support
   [*]    Bluetooth subsystem support
```

2. There are two main protocol selections for Bluetooth. Both of these should be enabled in order to work with all types of Bluetooth devices:

```
Networking
   [*] Networking support
      --- Bluetooth subsystem support
      [*]    L2CAP protocol support
      [*]    SCO links support
```

3. There are relatively few individual Bluetooth devices drivers available, because almost all of these devices follow the Bluetooth specification detailing how devices should operate. The drivers marked in the following list must be selected in order for Bluetooth to work with the device:

```
Networking
   [*] Networking support
      --- Bluetooth subsystem support
```

```
Bluetooth device drivers
    [M] HCI USB driver
    [*]   SCO (voice) support
    [ ] HCI UART driver
    [M] HCI BCM203x USB driver
    [M] HCI BPA10x USB driver
    [ ] HCI BlueFRITZ! USB driver
    [ ] HCI DTL1 (PC Card) driver
    [ ] HCI BT3C (PC Card) driver
    [ ] HCI BlueCard (PC Card) driver
    [ ] HCI UART (PC Card) device driver
    [ ] HCI VHCI (Virtual HCI device) driver
```

Wireless

Wireless networking is very popular, with almost all modern laptops having a built-in wireless network device. Linux supports a wide range of wireless drivers, with more being added every week. To determine whether you have a PCI wireless device on the system, and what type it is, run the following command:

```
$ /usr/sbin/lspci | grep -i wireless
06:05.0 Network controller: Intel Corporation PRO/Wireless 2915ABG MiniPCI
Adapter (rev 05)
```

Note that your response will probably not be identical; what is important is that the command shows some PCI wireless devices.

1. To enable wireless support in Linux, the IEEE 802.11 network configuration option must be enabled. (802.11 is the number of the wireless specification that all these devices follow.)

   ```
   Networking
       [*] Networking support
       [*]   Generic IEEE 802.11 Networking Stack
   ```

2. Also enable the different 802.11 protocol options and the Software MAC option to provide full support for all different types of wireless devices in Linux:

   ```
   Networking
       [*] Networking support
       [*]   Generic IEEE 802.11 Networking Stack
       [*]     IEEE 802.11 WEP encryption (802.1x)
       [M]     IEEE 802.11i CCMP support
       [M]     IEEE 802.11i TKIP encryption
       [M]     Software MAC add-on to the IEEE 802.11 networking stack
   ```

3. Support for the different PCI types of wireless network devices is found under the Network driver section of the configuration:

   ```
   Device Drivers
       Network device support
           Wireless LAN (non-hamradio)
               [*] Wireless LAN drivers (non-hamradio) & Wireless
               Extensions
               [*]   Wireless Extension API over RtNetlink
   ```

   There is a wide range of different PCI drivers in this section. Select the proper one depending on the device you have.

The USB wireless networking device drivers are in a different section of the configuration:

```
Device Drivers
    USB Support
        USB Network Adapters
```

Filesystems

Linux supports a wide range of traditional filesystem types and a number of different types of filesystems (volume managers, clustered filesystems, etc.). The traditional filesystem types (normal or journaled) can be selected from the main File systems configuration menu:

```
File systems
    [*] Second extended fs support
    [*] Ext3 journalling file system support
    [ ] Reiserfs support
    [ ] JFS filesystem support
    [ ] XFS filesystem support
```

This section will show a few of the nontraditional filesystem types that Linux supports and how to enable them.

RAID

RAID offers the option of combining numerous disks together so that they look like one logical disk. This can help in providing ways of providing redundancy or speed by spreading the data across different disk platters. Linux supports both hardware and software RAID. Hardware RAID is handled by the disk controller, without any help needed from the kernel.

1. Software RAID is controlled by the kernel, and can be selected as a build option:

```
Device Drivers
    Multi-device support (RAID and LVM)
        [*] Multiple devices driver support (RAID and LVM)
        [*]    RAID support
```

2. There are many different types of RAID configurations. At least one needs to be selected in order for RAID to work properly:

```
Device Drivers
    Multi-device support (RAID and LVM)
        [*] Multiple devices driver support (RAID and LVM)
        [*]    RAID support
        [*]        Linear (append) mode
        [*]        RAID-0 (striping) mode
        [*]        RAID-1 (mirroring) mode
        [*]        RAID-10 (mirrored striping) mode (EXPERIMENTAL)
        [*]        RAID-4/RAID-5 mode
        [*]        RAID-6 mode
```

Logical Volume Manager and Device Mapper

Much like RAID, Logical Volume Manager (LVM) allows the user to combine different block devices to look like one logical device. However, it does not work on a device level like RAID, but through a block and sector mapping mechanism. It allows different portions of different disks to be combined together to look like one large block device to the user. To do this, the kernel uses something called Device Mapper (DM).

1. Enable DM support in the kernel:

```
Device Drivers
    Multi-device support (RAID and LVM)
        [*] Multiple devices driver support (RAID and LVM)
        [*]   Device mapper support
```

2. There are a number of helper modules that work with DM to provide additional functionality. You should enable them if you wish to encrypt your devices, or allow snapshot functionality:

```
Device Drivers
    Multi-device support (RAID and LVM)
        [*] Multiple devices driver support (RAID and LVM)
        [*]   Device mapper support
        [*]     Crypt target support
        [*]     Snapshot target (EXPERIMENTAL)
        [*]     Mirror target (EXPERIMENTAL)
        [*]     Zero target (EXPERIMENTAL)
        [*]     Multipath target (EXPERIMENTAL)
```

File Sharing with Windows

Samba is a program that allows Linux users to access Windows machines natively across the network, providing a way to share drives and devices in a transparent manner. It also allows Linux to work as a Windows server, allowing Windows clients to connect to it thinking that it is a real Windows machine.

Two different filesystems that allow a Linux machine to connect with a Windows machine: the SMB filesystem and the CIFS filesystem. For the ability to connect to older Windows for Workgroups or Windows 95 or 98 machines, select the SMB filesystem:

```
File systems
    Network File Systems
        [*] SMB file system support (to mount Windows shares etc.)
```

For the ability to connect to newer Windows machines, the CIFS filesystem is recommended instead:

```
File systems
    Network File Systems
        [*] CIFS support
```

For more details on the differences between these two filesystems, and when one should be used instead of the other, please see the SMB_FS and CIFS entries in Chapter 11.

OCFS2

OCFS2 is a cluster filesystem from Oracle that works for large network installations and small local systems at the same time. This filesystem is recommended when using large databases, such as Oracle or DB2, because it can be moved over time to different backing disks across the network quite easily as more storage is needed.

To enable the filesystem:

```
File systems
    [*] OCFS2 file system support
```

Security

The Linux kernel supports different security models by providing hooks and letting you build in your choice of model. At the moment, only a few models come with the default kernel source tree, but developers of new models are working on getting more accepted.

Default Linux Capabilities

The standard type of security model for Linux is the "capability" model. You should always select this option unless you really want to run an insecure kernel for some reason.

To enable it:

```
Security options
    [*] Enable different security models
    [*]   Default Linux Capabilities
```

SELinux

A very popular security model is called SELinux. This model is supported by a number of different Linux distributions.

SELinux requires that the networking option be enabled. See the earlier section, "Networking," to enable this.

SELinux also requires that audit be enabled in the kernel configuration. To do this:

```
General setup
    [*] Auditing support
```

Also, the networking security option must be enabled:

```
Security options
    [*] Enable different security models
    [*]   Socket and Networking Security Hooks
```

Now it is possible to select the SELinux option:

```
Security options
    [*] Enable different security models
    [*] NSA SELinux Support
```

There are also a number of individual SELinux options that you might wish to enable. Please see the help for the individual different items for more descriptions on what they do:

```
Security options
    [*] Enable different security models
    [*] NSA SELinux Support
    [ ]     NSA SELinux boot parameter
    [ ]     NSA SELinux runtime disable
    [*]     NSA SELinux Development Support
    [*]     NSA SELinux AVC Statistics
    (1)     NSA SELinux checkreqprot default value
```

Kernel Debugging

A wide range of different kernel options can help in debugging what is going on within the kernel. Following is a list of some of the more common ones that can be useful for discovering new things about how the kernel works, or help find potential problems within the current kernel source code.

Kernel Log Timestamps

The kernel outputs a wide range of messages to its logfile. These messages can be seen by looking at the system logfile (usually located in *lvar/log/messages*), or by running the *dmesg* command.

Sometimes it is useful to see exactly when those messages were created. *dmesg*, however, does not put any timestamps on the events it shows, and the time resolution of *lvar/log/messages* is only to the nearest second. You can configure the kernel to assign each message a timestamp that is accurate down to the smallest measurable kernel time value (usually in the microsecond range).

To enable timestamp options on kernel messages:

```
Kernel hacking
    [*] Show timing information on printks
```

Magic SysRq Keys

The SysRq key on the keyboard can be used to control the kernel in a number of different ways while the kernel is running, or after it has crashed.

To enable this option:

```
Kernel hacking
    [*] Magic SysRq key
```

For a full description of the different actions that can be triggered by this option, please see the file *Documentation/sysrq.txt* in the kernel source tree.

Debug Filesystem

A RAM-based filesystem can be used to output a lot of different debugging information. This filesystem is called *debugfs* and can be enabled:

```
Kernel hacking
    [*] Debug filesystem
```

After you enable this option and boot the rebuilt kernel, it creates the directory */sys/kernel/debug* as a location for the user to mount the debugfs filesystem. Do this manually by:

```
$ mount -t debugfs none /sys/kernel/debug
```

Or have the filesystem mounted automatically at boot time by adding the following line to the */etc/fstab* file:

```
debugfs /sys/kernel/debug debugfs 0 0
```

After you mount *debugfs*, a large number of different directories and files will turn up in the */sys/kernel/debug/* directory. These are all virtual and dynamically generated by the kernel, like the files in *procfs* or *sysfs*. The files can be used to help debug different kernel subsystems, or just to see what is happening to the system as it runs.

General Kernel Debugging

Here are a range of other good kernel configuration options that you might wish to enable if you want to help kernel developers debug different problems, or just learn more about how the kernel works by looking at the messages that these options print out. Note that if you enable almost any of these options, the kernel will slow down a small amount, so if you notice any decrease in performance, you might wish to disable the options:

```
Kernel hacking
    [*] Kernel debugging
    [*]   Detect Soft Lockups
    [ ]   Collect scheduler statistics
    [*]   Debug slab memory allocations
    [*]     Memory leak debugging
    [*]   Mutex debugging, deadlock detection
    [*]   Spinlock debugging
    [*]   Sleep-inside-spinlock checking
    [ ]   kobject debugging
    [ ]   Highmem debugging
    [ ]   Compile the kernel with debug info
```

III

Kernel Reference

This section provides reference information on kernel parameters of all types.

9

Kernel Boot Command-Line Parameter Reference

The majority of this chapter is based on the in-kernel documentation for the different kernel boot command-line reference options, which were written by the kernel developers and released under the GPL.

There are three ways to pass options to the kernel and thus control its behavior:

- When building the kernel. Most of this book discusses these options.
- When starting the kernel. Usually, parameters are passed to the kernel when it is invoked from a boot file such as the GRUB or LILO configuration file.
- At runtime, by writing to files in the */proc* and */sys* directories.

This chapter describes the second method of passing options. The chapter breaks the boot time options into different logical sections. A number of architecture-specific and individual driver options are not listed here. For a complete list of all known options, please see the file *Documentation/kernel-parameters.txt* in the kernel source tree and the individual architecture-specific documentation files.

Not all of the listed options are always available. Most are associated with subsystems and work only if the kernel is configured with those subsystems built in. They also depend on the presence of the hardware with which they are associated.

All of these parameters are case-sensitive.

Module-Specific Options

In addition to the options listed in this chapter, parameters for modules that are built in to the kernel can also be passed on the command line. (Dynamically loaded modules, of course, are not in memory when the kernel boots and therefore cannot be passed as parameters at boot time.) The syntax for passing parameters consists of the module name followed by a dot (.) and the parameter.

For example, the *usbcore* module accepts the parameter *blinkenlights* to display flashing lights on all supported USB 2.0 hubs (don't ever say the kernel developers don't have a sense of humor). To set this parameter when loading the module dynamically, you would enter:

```
$ modprobe usbcore blinkenlights=1
```

But if the *usbcore* module is built into the kernel, you achieve the same effect by invoking the kernel with the following option:

```
usbcore.blinkenlights=1
```

Most module options for modules that are built into the kernel can also be changed at runtime by writing to files in the subdirectory named after the module under the */sys/module* directory. Thus, the *blinkenlights* option is represented by the file */sys/module/usbcore/blinkenlights*.

Console Options

These options deal with the console or kernel log, where kernel debugging and error information are displayed.

---

console
Output console device and options.

```
console=Options
```

tty*n*
> Use the virtual console device *n*.

ttyS*n*[,*options*], ttyUSB0[,*options*]
> Use the specified serial port. The options are of the form *bbbbpnf*, where *bbbb* is the baud rate, *p* is parity (n, o, or e), *n* is number of bits, and *f* is flow control (r for RTS or omitted). Default is 9600n8.
>
> See the file *Documentation/serial-console.txt* for more information on how to use a serial console. If you wish to have access to the kernel console information and do not have a serial port, see the *netconsole* command-line option.

uart,io,*addr*[,*options*], uart,mmio,*addr*[,*options*]
> Start an early, polled-mode console on the 8250/16550 UART at the specified I/O port or MMIO address, switching to the specified ttyS device later. The options are the same as for ttyS shown earlier.

---

netconsole
Output console data across the network.

```
netconsole=[src-port]@[src-ip]/[dev],[target-port]@target-ip/[target-mac-address]
```

Send kernel console data across the network using UDP packets to another machine. Options are:

---

src-port
> Source port for the UDP packets. The default value is 6665.

src-ip
> Source IP address of the interface to use.

dev
> Network interface to use. eth0 is an example. The network interface can also run normal network traffic, because the netconsole data is not intrusive and should cause no slow-down in other network operations.

target-port
> Port that the logging agent will use. The default value is 6666.

target-ip
> IP address for the logging agent.

target-mac-address
> Ethernet MAC address for the logging agent.

To listen to this data, the remote machine can use the *syslogd* program, or run the *netcat* program as follows:

```
netcat -u -l -p port
```

For more background on how to use this option, see the file *Documentation/networking/netconsole.txt*.

---

debug

Enable kernel debugging.

Cause the kernel log level to be set to the debug level, so that all debug messages will be printed to the console at boot time.

---

quiet

Disable all log messages.

Set the default kernel log level to KERN_WARNING (4), which suppresses all messages during boot except extremely serious ones. (Log levels are defined under the *loglevel* parameter.)

---

earlyprintk

Show early boot messages.

```
earlyprintk=[vga|serial][,ttySn[,baudrate]][,keep]
```

Show kernel log messages that precede the initialization of the traditional console. These messages are typically never seen on the console unless you use this option. Enabling this can be very useful for tracking down hardware issues. Currently, the option can specify either the VGA device or the serial port, but not both at the same time. Also, only the ttyS0 or ttyS1 serial devices will work. Interaction with the standard serial driver is not very good, and the VGA output will eventually be overwritten by the real console.

Append ,keep in order not to disable the messages shown by this option when the real kernel console is initialized and takes over the system.

loglevel

Set the default console log level.

```
loglevel=level
```

Specify the initial console log level. Any log messages with levels less than this (that is, of higher priority) will be printed to the console, whereas any messages with levels equal to or greater than this will not be displayed.

The console log level can also be changed by the *klogd* program, or by writing the specified level to the */proc/sys/kernel/printk* file.

The kernel log levels are:

0 (KERN_EMERG)
: The system is unusable.

1 (KERN_ALERT)
: Actions that must be taken care of immediately.

2 (KERN_CRIT)
: Critical conditions.

3 (KERN_ERR)
: Noncritical error conditions.

4 (KERN_WARNING)
: Warning conditions that should be taken care of.

5 (KERN_NOTICE)
: Normal, but significant events.

6 (KERN_INFO)
: Informational messages that require no action.

7 (KERN_DEBUG)
: Kernel debugging messages, output by the kernel if the developer enabled debugging at compile time.

log_buf_len

Set the size of the kernel log buffer.

```
log_buf_len=n[KMG]
```

Set the size of the kernel's internal log buffer. *n* must be a power of 2, if not, it will be rounded up to be a power of 2. This value can also be changed by the CONFIG_LOG_BUF_SHIFT kernel configuration value.

initcall_debug

Debug the initcall functions in the kernel.

Cause the kernel to trace all functions that are called by the kernel during initialization of the system as the kernel boots. This option is useful for determining where the kernel is dying during startup.

kstack	How many words of the stack to print in kernel oopses.
	`kstack=n`
	Specify how many words from the kernel stack should be printed in the kernel oops dumps. *n* is an integer value.
time	Show timing data on every kernel log message.
	Cause the kernel to prefix every kernel log message with a timestamp.

Interrupt Options

Interrupts are a complex aspect of kernel behavior. The boot time options deal mostly with the interface between the kernel and the hardware that handles interrupts, such as the Intel chip's Advanced Programmable Interrupt Controller (APIC).

apic	Change the verbosity of the APIC subsystem when booting.
	`apic=[quiet|verbose|debug]`
	Control how much information the APIC subsystem generates when booting the kernel. The default is `quiet`.
noapic	Do not use any IOAPICs.
	Prevent the kernel from using any of the IOAPICs that might be present in the system.
lapic	Enable the local APIC.
	Cause the kernel to enable the local APIC even if the BIOS had disabled it.
nolapic	Do not use the local APIC.
	Tell the kernel not to use the local APIC.
noirqbalance	Disable kernel IRQ balancing.
	Disable all of the built-in kernel IRQ balancing logic.

irqfixup

Basic fix to interrupt problems.

When an interrupt is not handled, search all known interrupt handlers for it. This is intended to get systems with badly broken firmware running.

irqpoll

Extended fix to interrupt problems.

When an interrupt is not handled, search all known interrupt handlers for it and also check all handlers on each timer interrupt. This is intended to get systems with badly broken firmware running.

noirqdebug

Disable unhandled interrupt detection.

By default, the kernel attempts to detect and disable unhandled interrupt sources because they can cause problems with the responsiveness of the rest of the kernel if left unchecked. This option disables this logic.

Memory Options

The kernel handles memory in many different chunks and categories for different purposes. These options allow you to tweak the sizes and settings.

highmem

Specify the size of the highmem memory zone.

highmem=n

Force the highmem memory zone to have an exact size of n bytes. This will work even on boxes that have no highmem zones by default. It can also reduce the size of the highmem zone for machines with a lot of memory.

hugepages

Set the number of hugetlb pages.

hugepages=n

The hugetlb feature lets you configure Linux to use 4 MB pages, one thousand times the default size. If Linux is configured this way, this options sets the maximum number of hugetlb pages to be n.

ihash_entries   Set the number of inode hash buckets.

ihash_entries=*n*

Override the default number of hash buckets for the kernel's inode cache. Recommended only for kernel experts.

---

max_addr   Ignore memory.

max_addr=*n*

Cause the kernel to ignore all physical memory greater than or equal to the physical address *n*.

---

mem   Force memory usage.

mem=*n*[KMG]

Set the specific ammount of memory used by the kernel. When used with the memmap= option, physical address space collisions can be avoided. Without the memmap= option, this option could cause PCI devices to be placed at addresses that belong to unused RAM. *n* specifies the amount of memory to force and is measured in units of kilobytes (K), megabytes (M), or gigabytes (G).

---

mem   Disable the use of 4 MB pages for kernel memory.

mem=nopentium

Disable the use of huge (4 MB) pages for kernel memory.

---

memmap   Enable setting of an exact E820 memory map.

memmap=*exactmap*

Use a specific memory map. The *exactmap* lines can be constructed based on BIOS output or other requirements.

---

memmap   Force specific memory to be used.

memmap=*n*[KMG]@*start*[KMG]

Force the kernel to use a specific memory region. *n* is the size of the memory location, and *start* is the start location in memory of the range. Units can be kilobytes (K), megabytes (M), or gigabytes (G).

noexec

Enable or disable nonexecutable mappings.

noexec=[on|off]

Enable or disable the kernel's ability to map sections of memory as nonexecutable. By default, the mapping is enabled (on).

reserve

Reserve some I/O memory.

reserve=*n*[KMG]

Force the kernel to ignore some of the I/O memory areas.

vmalloc

Force the vmalloc area to have a specific size.

vmalloc=*n*[KMG]

Force *vmalloc* to have the exact size specified by *n*. This can be used to increase the minimum size of the *vmalloc* area (which is 128 MB on the x86 processor). It can also be used to decrease the size and leave more room for directly mapped kernel RAM.

norandmaps

Do not use address space randomization.

By default, the kernel randomizes the address space of all programs when they are started. This option disables this feature. It is equivalent to writing 0 to the file */proc/sys/kernel/randomize_va_space*.

vdso

Enable or disable the VDSO mapping.

vdso=[0|1]

Disable (0) or enable (1) the VDSO (Virtual Dynamic Shared Object) mapping option. By default, it is enabled.

Suspend Options

These options change the way the kernel handles suspension for power-saving purposes.

resume

Specify the partition device for the suspend image.

resume=*suspend_device*

Tell the kernel which disk device contains the suspended kernel image. If the data on the image is a valid kernel image created by the software suspend subsystem, it will be loaded into memory and the kernel will run it instead of continuing on with the normal boot process. *suspend_device* is the kernel device name, which might be different from what userspace thinks the device name is, so be careful with this option.

noresume   Disable resume.

Disable the resume functionality of the kernel. Any swap partitions that were being used to hold system images to which the kernel could be restored will revert back to available swap space.

CPU Options

These options control a wide range of behavior regarding timing, processor use in multiprocessor systems, and other processor issues.

cachesize   Override level 2 CPU cache size detection.

```
cachesize=n
```

Sometimes CPU hardware bugs make them report the cache size incorrectly. The kernel will attempt to work around and fix known problems with most CPUs, but for some CPUs it is not possible to determine what the correct size should be. This option provides an override for these situations. *n* is measured in bytes.

lpj   Set the loops per jiffy.

```
lpg=n
```

Specify the loops per jiffy that should be used by the kernel, and thus have the kernel avoid the time-consuming boot-time autodetection of this value. If *n* is 0, the value will be autodetected as usual.

On SMP systems, this value will be set on all CPUs, which might cause problems if the different CPUs need different settings. An incorrect value will cause incorrect delays in the kernel, which can lead to unpredictable I/O errors and other breakage. Although unlikely, in extreme cases this might damage your hardware.

nmi_watchdog	Set the NMI watchdog value.

nmi_watchdog=[0|1|2|3]

This is a debugging feature that allows the user to override the default nonmaskable interrupt (NMI) watchdog value. 0 specifies that no NMI watchdog should be used. 1 specifies that the APIC should be used if present. 2 specifies that the local APIC should be used if present. 3 means that the NMI watchdog is invalid, so do not use it.

no387	Always use the 387 emulation library.

Always use the 387 math emulation library, even if a 387 math coprocessor is present in the system.

nofxsr	Disable x86 floating-point save and restore.

Disable the x86 floating-point extended register save and restore. The kernel will save only legacy floating-point registers on a task switch.

no-hlt	Do not use the HLT instruction.

This option is available because the HLT instruction does not work correctly for some x86 processors. This option tells the kernel not to use the instruction.

mce	Enable the machine check exception feature.

Some processors can check for machine errors (usually errors in the hardware). This option turns this subsystem on, if it has been built into the kernel configuration.

nomce	Disable the machine check exception feature.

This option turns the subsystem off.

nosep	Disable x86 SYSENTER/SYSEXIT support.

Disable x86 SYSENTER/SYSEXIT support in the kernel. This can cause some system calls to take longer.

nosmp	Run as a single-processor machine.

Tell an SMP kernel to act as a uniprocessor kernel, even on a multi-processor machine.

notsc   Disable the time stamp counter.

Disable the timestamp counter hardware in the system, if present.

max_cpus   Maximum number of CPUs to use.

maxcpus=*n*

Specify the maximum number of processors that a SMP kernel should use, even if there are more processors present in the system.

Scheduler Options

These options tweak the parameters used to make scheduling decisions. Most depend on an intimate understanding of how scheduling works in Linux.

isolcpus   Isolate CPUs from the kernel scheduler.

isolcpus=*cpu_number*[,*cpu_number*,...]

Remove the specified CPUs, as defined by the *cpu_number* values, from the general kernel SMP balancing and scheduler algroithms. The only way to move a process onto or off an "isolated" CPU is via the CPU affinity syscalls. *cpu_number* begins at 0, so the maximum value is one less than the number of CPUs on the system.

This option is the preferred way to isolate CPUs. The alternative, manually setting the CPU mask of all tasks in the system, can cause problems and suboptimal load-balancer performance.

migration_cost   Override the default scheduler migrations costs.

migration_cost=*level-1-useconds*[*level-2-useconds*...]

This is a debugging option that overrides the default scheduler migration cost matrix. The numbers specified by *level-N-useconds* are indexed by the "CPU domain distance" and are measured in microseconds.

An example of this option is migration_cost=1000,2000,3000 for a SMT NUMA machine. It sets up an intra-core migration cost of 1 ms, another inter-core migration cost of 2 ms, and another inter-node migration cost of 3 ms.

Incorrect values can severely degrade scheduler performance, so this option should be used only for scheduler development, never for production environments.

migration_ debug	Verbosity of migration cost autodetection. `migration_debug=[0|1|2]`

Set the migration cost debug level. If 0 is specified, no extra messages will be printed to the kernel log. This is the default value. 1 prints some information on how the matrix is determined. 2 is very verbose and is useful only if you use a serial console, as the amount of information will overflow the kernel log buffer.

migration_ factor	Multiply or divide the migration costs. `migration_factor=percent`

Modify the default migration costs by the specified *percent*. This is a debugging option that can be used to proportionally increase or decrease the autodetected migration costs for all entries of the migration matrix. For example, `migration_factor=150` increases migration costs by 50 percent, so the scheduler will be less eager to migrate cache-hot tasks. `migration_factor=80` decreases migration costs by 20 percent, thus making the scheduler more eager to migrate tasks.

Incorrect values can severely degrade scheduler performance, so this option should be used only for scheduler development, never for production environments.

Ramdisk Options

These options control how the storage of information in memory used to imitate disks (ramdisks) is done, including init ramdisks that hold information necessary at some stages of booting.

initrd	Location of initial ramdisk. `initrd=filename`

Specify where the initial ramdisk for the kernel boot is located.

load_ramdisk	Load a kernel ramdisk from a floppy. `load_ramdisk=n`

If *n* is set to 1, a ramdisk is loaded by the kernel at boot time from the floppy drive.

noinitrd	Do not use any initrd.

Do not load any initial ramdisk, even if it is configured in other options passed to the kernel.

prompt_ramdisk	Prompt for the list of ramdisks.

```
prompt_ramdisk=1
```

Prompt the user for the initial ramdisk before attempting to read it from the floppy drive.

ramdisk_blocksize	Blocksize of the ramdisk.

```
ramdisk_blocksize=n
```

Tell the ramdisk driver how many bytes to use per block. The default size is 1,024.

ramdisk_size	Size of the ramdisk.

```
ramdisk_size=n
```

Specify the size of the initial ramdisk in kilobytes. The default size is 4,096 (4 MB). This option should be used instead of the older *ramdisk* command-line option.

Root Disk Options

These options control how the kernel finds and handles the filesystem that contains the root filesystem.

ro	Mount the root device read-only on boot.

The default for the kernel is to mount the root device as read-only at boot time. This option ensures that this is the mode the kernel uses. It overrides the rw command-line option, if it had been specified earlier on the boot command line.

root	Specify the root filesystem to boot from.

```
root=device
```

Tell the kernel which disk device the root filesystem image is on. *device* can be specified in one of the following ways:

nnnn

A device number in hexadecimal represents the major and minor number of the device in the internal format that the kernel expects. This method is not recommended unless you have access to kernel internals.

`/dev/nfs`

Use the NFS disk specified by the `nfsroot` boot option as the root disk.

`/dev/<diskname>`

Use the kernel disk name specified by *<diskname>* as the root disk.

`/dev/<diskname><decimal>`

Use the kernel disk name specified by *<diskname>* and the partition specified by *<decimal>* as the root disk.

`/dev/<diskname>p<decimal>`

Use the kernel disk name specified by *<diskname>* and the partition specified by *<decimal>* as the root disk. This is the same as above, but is needed when *<diskname>* ends with a digit.

---

rootdelay   Time to delay before attempting to mount the root filesystem.

`rootdelay=n`

Wait *n* seconds before trying to mount the root filesystem. This can be useful if the root filesystem is on a USB or FireWire device, as those disk devices take a bit longer to be discovered by the kernel.

---

rootflags   The root filesystem mount options.

`rootflags=options`

Mount options that the kernel should use in mounting the root filesystem. The *options* value depend on the filesystem type; see the documentation for the individual types for details on what is valid.

---

rootfstype   The root filesystem type.

`rootfstype=type`

Try to mount the root filesystem as this type of filesystem. For instance, `rootfstype=ext3`.

---

rw   Mount the root device read-write on boot.

The default for the kernel is to mount the root device as read-only at boot time. This option mounts the root device as read-write instead.

Init Options

The *init* process is the first to be started by the kernel and is the ancestor of all other processes. These options control which program is run and how it is run.

init	Program to run at init time.

init=*filename*

Run the specified binary as the *init* process instead of the default */sbin/init* program.

rdinit	Run the *init* process from the ramdisk.

rdinit=*full_path_name*

Run the program specified by *full_path_name* as the *init* process. This file must be on the kernel ramdisk instead of on the root filesystem.

S	Run *init* in single-user mode.

The default for the kernel is to run *init* in multi-user mode. This option runs *init* in single-user mode instead.

kexec Options

The kexec subsystem is a specialized rebooting feature that allows a fast reboot and is usually combined with the kdump facility that enables the previous kernel's memory to be dumped to a safe place for analysis at a later time. These options modify the kexec subsystem's parameters.

crashkernel	Reserve a portion of physical memory for kexec to use.

crashkernel=*n*[KMG]@*start*[KMG]

The kexec subsystem likes to have a portion of physical memory reserved for it. This option reserves that memory from the rest of the kernel and will switch to use it if the kernel panics. *n* specifies the amount of memory to reserve, and *start* specifies the location for this memory chunk. Both are measured in units of kilobytes (K), megabytes (M), or gigabytes (G).

elfcorehdr	Start of the kernel core image ELF header.

```
elfcorhdr=n
```

The kernel, like every Linux executable, is stored in ELF format. This option specifies the physical address where the kernel core image's ELF header starts. This is used by kexec to find the kernel when booting the secondary kernel image.

RCU Options

Read Copy Update (RCU) is a portion of the kernel that handles mutual exclusion for a variety of subsystems in a lockless manner. There are a number of options that can be used to tune RCU in different ways:

rcu.blimit	RCU batch limit.

```
rcu.blimit=n
```

Set the maximum number of finished RCU callbacks to process in one batch.

rcu.qhimark	RCU queue high level.

```
rcu.qhimark=n
```

Batch limiting is disabled when the number of queued RCU callbacks rises above *n*.

rcu.qlowmark	RCU queue low level.

```
rcu.qlowmark=n
```

Batch limiting is re-enabled when the number of queued RCU callbacks falls below *n*.

rcu.rsinterval	RCU callback queue length.

```
rcu.rsinterval=n
```

Set the number of additional RCU callbacks that should be queued before forcing a reschedule on all CPUs.

ACPI Options

These options control parameters that the Advanced Configuration and Power Interface (ACPI) subsystem can use.

---

acpi ACPI subsystem options.

```
acpi=[force|off|noirq|ht|strict]
```

This is the main option for the Advanced Configuration and Power Interface (ACPI). Values are:

force
> Force ACPI to be enabled. Can be used to override the kernel configuration option that disabled it.

off
> Disable ACPI. Can be used to override the kernel configuration option that enabled it.

noirq
> Prevent ACPI from being used for IRQ routing.

ht
> Run only enough of the ACPI layer to enable HyperThreading on processors that are capable of it.

strict
> Make the ACPI layer be less tolerant of platforms that are not fully compliant with the ACPI specification.

---

acpi_sleep ACPI sleep options.

```
acpi_sleep=[s3_bios],[s3_mode]
```

During S3 resume (which happens after the machine has been suspended to RAM), hardware needs to be reinitialized properly. For most devices this is simple, except for video cards, which are normally initialized by the BIOS. The kernel does not have enough information to restore the video device, because that information is in the BIOS and not accessable at all. This option lets the kernel try to use the ACPI subsystem to restore the video card in two different ways.

See the file *Documentation/power/video.txt* for more information on this option and how to find the proper value for your type of hardware.

---

acpi_sci ACPI System Control Interrupt trigger mode.

```
acpi_sci=[level|edge|high|low]
```

Set the ACPI System Control Interrupt trigger mode.

acpi_irq_balance	Enable ACPI IRQ balance.
	Cause ACPI to balance the active IRQs. This is the default option when operating in APIC mode.

acpi_irq_nobalance	Disable ACPI IRQ balance.
	Cause ACPI not to move the active IRQs. This is the default option when operating in PIC mode.

acpi_irq_isa	Mark the listed IRQs as used by ISA.
	`acpi_irq_isa=irq[,irq...]`
	If the IRQ balance option is enabled, mark the listed IRQs as used by the ISA subsystem.

acpi_irq_pci	Mark the listed IRQs as used by PCI.
	`acpi_irq_pci=irq[,[irq...]`
	If the IRQ balance option is enabled, mark the listed IRQs as used by the PCI subsystem.

acpi_os_name	Fake the operating system name to ACPI.
	`acpi_os_name=name`
	Tell the ACPI BIOS that the name of the running operating system is *name*. This can be useful to spoof the BIOS into thinking that Windows is running instead of Linux, which can help solve some ACPI issues for older BIOSes. As an example, use the string `Microsoft 2001` to spoof the BIOS into thinking that Windows 2001 is running on the machine.

acpi_osi	Disable the _OSI ACPI method.
	`acpi_osi=[n]`
	This is actually a binary option despite the integer value. If *n* is absent, ACPI will disable the _OSI method. If *n* is present, _OSI will not be disabled.

acpi_serialize	Force serialization of AML methods.
	Force the serialization of ACPI Machine Language methods.

| **acpi_skip_ timer_override** | Skip interrupt override issues. |
| | Allow the ACPI layer to recognize and ignore IRQ0/pin2 interrupt override issues for broken nForce2 BIOSes that result in the XT-PIC timer acting up. |

| **acpi_dbg_layer** | ACPI debug layer. |

```
acpi_dbg_layer=n
```

Set the ACPI debug layers. *n* is an integer in which each bit indicates a different ACPI debug layer. After the system has booted, the debug layers can be set via the */proc/acpi/debug_layer* file.

| **acpi_fake_ecdt** | ECDT workaround. |

If present, this allows ACPI to workaround BIOS failures when it lacks an Embedded Controller Description Table.

| **acpi_generic_ hotkey** | Use generic ACPI hotkey driver. |

This allows the ACPI consolidated generic hotkey driver to override the platform-specific driver if one is present.

| **acpi_pm_good** | Override pmtimer bug detection. |

Force the kernel to assume that the machine's pmtimer latches its value and always returns good values.

| **ec_intr** | ACPI Embedded Controller interrupt mode. |

```
ec_intr=n
```

Specify the ACPI embedded controller interrupt mode. If *n* is 0, polling mode will be used, otherwise interrupt mode will be used. Interrupt mode is the default.

| **memmap** | Mark specific memory as ACPI data. |

```
memmap=n[KMG]#start[KMG]
```

Marks a specific location and range of memory as ACPI data. *n* is the size of the memory location and *start* is the start location in memory of the range. Both are measured in units of kilobytes (K), megabytes (M), or gigabytes (G).

| **memmap** | Mark specific memory as reserved. |

memmap=n[KMG]$start[KMG]

This marks a specific location and range of memory as reserved. *n* is the size of the memory location and *start* is the start location in memory of the range.

| **pnpacpi** | Turn Plug and Play ACPI off. |

pnpacpi=off

Disable the Plug and Play ACPI functionality.

| **processor.max_ cstate** | Limit the processor to a maximum C-state. |

processor.max_cstate=n

Limit the processor to a maximum C-state, no matter what the ACPI tables say it can support. *n* is a valid C-state value. A value of 9 overrides any DMI blacklist limit that might be present for this processor.

| **processor.nocst** | Ignore the _CST method for C-states. |

Causes the ACPI core to ignore the _CST method of determining the processor C-states and use the legacy FADT method instead.

SCSI Options

These options specify different parameters the SCSI subsystem can use. A number of SCSI driver-specific options are also available; please see the different driver documentation files in the kernel directory *Documentation/scsi/* for details.

| **max_luns** | Maximum number of SCSI LUNS to probe. |

max_luns=n

Specify the maximum number of SCSI LUNS that the system should probe. *n* is an integer from 1 to 4,294,967,295.

| **max_report_ luns** | Maximum number of SCSI LUNS received. |

max_report_luns=n

Specify the maximum number of SCSI LUNs that the system can receive. *n* is an integer from 1 to 16,384.

| **scsi_dev_flags** | SCSI black/white list. |

```
scsi_dev_flags=vendor:model:flags
```

This option lets the user add entries to the SCSI black/white list for a specific vendor and model of device.

PCI Options

These options specify different parameters the PCI subsystem can use:

| **PCI** | `pci=option[,option...]` |

Each *option* can be one of the following:

off
: Do not probe for the PCI bus.

bios
: Force the use of the PCI BIOS by not accessing the hardware directly. This means that the kernel should trust the BIOS, which is not the standard thing to do (as BIOSes are known to lie more often than they are known to be valid). Use this only if your machine has a nonstandard PCI host bridge and the normal boot method is not working properly.

nobios
: Do not use the PCI BIOS, but access the hardware directly instead. This is the default method of probing for PCI devices in all kernels after 2.6.13.

conf1
: Force use of PCI Configuration Mechanism 1 (a way to access PCI memory on i386 machines).

conf2
: Force use of PCI Configuration Mechanism 2 (a way to access PCI memory on i386 machines).

nommconf
: Disable use of the ACPI MMCONFIG table for PCI configuration.

nomsi
: If the PCI_MSI kernel config parameter is enabled, this kernel boot option can be used to disable the use of MSI interrupts system-wide.

nosort
: Do not sort PCI devices according to order given by the PCI BIOS. This sorting is done to get a device order compatible with much older kernel versions.

`biosirq`

Use PCI BIOS calls to get the interrupt routing table. These calls are known to be buggy on several machines and hang these machine when used, but on other machines they are the only way to get the interrupt routing table. Try this option if the kernel is unable to allocate IRQs or discover secondary PCI buses on your motherboard.

`rom`

Assign address space to expansion ROMs. Use this with caution as certain devices share address decoders between ROMs and other resources.

`irqmask=0xnnnn`

Set a bit mask of IRQs allowed to be assigned automatically to PCI devices. You can make the kernel exclude IRQs of your ISA cards this way.

`pirqaddr=0xn`

Specify the physical address of the PIRQ table (normally generated by the BIOS) if it is outside the F0000–100000 (hexadecimal) range.

`lastbus=n`

Scan all buses through bus *n*. Can be useful if the kernel is unable to find your secondary buses and you want to tell it explicitly which ones they are.

`assign-busses`

Always use your own PCI bus numbers, overriding whatever the firmware may have done.

`usepirqmask`

Honor the possible IRQ mask stored in the BIOS $PIR table. This is needed on some systems with broken BIOSes, notably some HP Pavilion N5400 and Omnibook XE3 notebooks. This will have no effect if ACPI IRQ routing is enabled.

`noacpi`

Do not use ACPI for IRQ routing or for PCI scanning.

`routeirq`

Do IRQ routing for all PCI devices. This is normally done in `pci_enable_device()`, so this option is a temporary workaround for broken drivers that don't call it.

`firmware`

Do not re-enumerate the bus, but instead just use the configuration from the bootloader. This is currently used on IXP2000 systems where the bus has to be configured a certain way for adjunct CPUs.

Plug and Play BIOS Options

noisapnp	Disable the ISA Plug and Play (PnP) subsystem.
	Disable the ISA PnP subsystem, if it has been enabled in the kernel configuration.

pnpbios	PnP BIOS settings.
	pnpbios=[on|off|curr|no-curr]
	Set the main PnP BIOS settings. on enables the PnP BIOS subsystem. off disables the PnP BIOS subsystem. curr tells the PnP BIOS subsystem to use the current static settings and no-curr tells the subsystem to probe for dynamic settings if possible.

pnp_reserve_ irq	PnP BIOS reserved IRQs.
	pnp_reserve_irq=irq1[,irq2...]
	List of the IRQs that the PnP BIOS subsystem should not use for autoconfiguration.

pnp_reserve_ dma	PnP BIOS reserved DMAs.
	pnp_reserve_dma=dma1[,dma2...]
	List of the DMAs that the PnP BIOS subsystem should not use for autoconfiguration.

pnp_reserve_io	PnP BIOS reserved I/O ports.
	pnp_reserve_io=io1,size1[,io2,size2...]
	I/O ports that the PnP BIOS subsystem should not use for autoconfiguration. Each port is listed by its starting location and size.

pnp_reserve_ mem	PnP BIOS reserved memory regions.
	pnp_reserve_mem=mem1,size1[,mem2,size2...]
	Memory regions that the PnP BIOS subsystem should not use for autoconfiguration. Each region is listed by its starting location and size.

Boot
Reference

SELinux Options

These options change some fundamental aspects of SELinux startup.

---

checkreqprot   Set the initial checkreqprot flag value.

```
checkreqprot=[0|1]
```

Set the initial *checkreqprot* flag value. 0 means that the check protection will be applied by the kernel and will include any implied execute protection. 1 means that the check protection is requested by the application. The default value is set by a kernel configuration option.

The value can be changed at runtime via the */selinux/checkreqprot* file.

---

enforcing   Set the initial enforcing status.

```
enforcing=[0|1]
```

Specify whether SELinux enforces its rules upon boot. 0 means that SELinux will just log policy violations but will not deny access to anything. 1 means that the enforcement will be fully enabled with denials as well as logging. The default value is 0.

The value can be changed at runtime via the */selinux/enforce* file.

---

selinux   Enable or disable SELinux at boot time.

```
selinux=[0|1]
```

This option allows SELinux to be enabled (1) or disabled (0) to boot time. The default value is set by a kernel configuration option.

If SELinux is enabled at boot time, the */selinux/disable* file can be used later to disable it prior to the initial policy load.

---

selinux_ compat_net   Set the network control model.

```
selinux_compat_net=[0|1]
```

Set the initial value for the SELinux network control model. 0 uses the new secmark-based packet controls, and 1 uses the legacy packet controls. 0 is the default and preferred value.

This value can be changed at runtime via the */selinux/compat_net* file.

Network Options

These options control low-level aspects of the networking subsystem.

netdev	Set various network device parameters.

netdev=[*irq*],[*io*],[*mem_start*],[*mem_end*],[*name*]

Specify network device parameters, which are specific to the driver used by the network device. Some drivers' source files document the applicable options. This option does not usually apply to PCI, USB, or other plug-and-play network devices. It is intended for use only on devices that can not discover their own resource assignments.

rhash_entries	Set the number of route cache hash buckets.

dhash_entries=*n*

This option lets you override the default number of hash buckets for the kernel's route cache. Recommended only for kernel network experts.

shapers	Set the maximum number of network shapers.

shapers=*n*

This option lets you set the maximum number of network shapers that the kernel can use.

thash_entries	Set the number of TCP connection hash buckets.

thash_entries=*n*

This option lets you override the default number of hash buckets for the kernel's TCP connection cache.

Network File System Options

These options control NFS startup.

lockd.nlm_ grace_period	Assign a grace period to the lock manager.

lockd.nlm_grace_period=*n*

Set the NFS lock manager grace period. *n* is measured in seconds.

lockd.nlm_tcpport

Assign a TCP port to the lock manager.

```
lockd.nlm_tcpport=port
```

Set the TCP port that the NFS lock manager should use. *port* must be a valid TCP port value.

lockd.nlm_timeout

Assign a new timeout value to the lock manager.

```
lockd.nlm_timeout=n
```

Override the default time value for the NFS lock manager. *n* is measured in seconds. If this option is not specified, the default of 10 seconds will be used.

lockd.nlm_udpport

Assign a UDP port to the lock manager.

```
lockd.nlm_udpport=port
```

Set the UDP port that the NFS lock manager should use. *port* must be a valid UDP port value.

nfsroot

Specifies the NFS root filesystem.

```
nfsroot=[server-ip:]root-dir[,nfs-options]
```

Set the NFS root filesystem for diskless boxes, to enable them to boot properly over NFS. If this parameter is not set, the value */tftp-boot/client_ip_address* will be used as the root filesystem with the default NFS options.

server-ip
: IP address of the NFS server to connect to.

root-dir
: Directory on the NFS server to mount as root. If there is a %s token in this string, it will be replaced with the ASCII representation of the client's IP address.

nfs-options
: The standard NFS options, such as ro, separated by commas.

nfs.callback_tcpport

Set the NFSv4 TCP port for the callback channel.

```
nfs.callback_tcpport=port
```

Specify the TCP port that the NFSv4 callback channel should listen on. *port* must be a valid TCP port value.

**nfs.idmap_
cache_timeout**   Set the maximum lifetime for idmapper cache entries.

`nfs.idmap_cache_timeout=n`

Specify the maximum lifetime for idmapper cache entries. *n* is measured in seconds.

Hardware-Specific Options

These options specify different parameters, depending on the hardware present in the system.

nousb   Disable the USB subsystem.

If this option is present, the USB subsystem will not be initialized.

lp   Parallel port and its mode.

`lp=[0|port[,port...]]|reset|auto]`

Specify the parallel port to use. The `lp=port1,port2...` format associates a sequence of parallel ports to devices, starting with lp0. An example is `lp=none,parport0`, which would suppress configuration of the lp0 device and cause the lp1 device to use the first parallel port.

`lp=0`
> Disables the printer driver.

`lp=reset`
> Causes the attached printers to be reset. This option can be combined with the port specifications.

`lp=auto`
> Causes the kernel to examine the device ID from each port to determine whether a IEEE 1284-compatible printer is attached. If so, the kernel will manage that printer.

parport   Specify the parallel port parameters.

`parport=[setting[,setting...]`

Specify settings for parallel port drivers. Parallel ports are assigned in the order they are specified on the command line, starting with parport0.

auto forces the driver to use any IRQ/DMA settings detected (the default is to ignore detected IRQ/DMA settings because of possible conflicts). You can also specify the base address, IRQ, and DMA settings in the format 0x*nnnn*[,*irq*[,*dma*]]. *irq* and *dma* can be numbers, auto to use detected settings on that particular port, or nofifo to avoid using a FIFO even if it is detected.

parport_init_ mode	Parallel port initialization mode. parport_init_mode=[spp|ps2|epp|ecp|ecpepp] Specifies the mode for operating the parallel port. This is necessary on the Pegasos computer where the firmware has no options for setting up the parallel port mode. This option works for parallel port chips of type 686a and 8231.
nr_uarts	Maximum number of UARTs to be registered. nr_uarts=*n* Specifies the maximum number of different UARTs that can be registered in the kernel.

Timer-Specific Options

These options override default kernel behavior to fix problems with certain chips.

enable_timer_ pin_1	Enable pin 1 of the APIC timer. Enable pin 1 of the APIC timer. This option can be useful to work around chipset bugs (on some ATI chipsets in particular). The kernel tries to set a reasonable default, but sometimes this option is necessary to override it.
disable_timer_ pin_1	Disable pin 1 of the APIC timer. Disable pin 1 of the APIC timer. Useful for the same reasons as enable_timer_pin_1.
enable_8254_ timer	Enable interrupt 0 timer routing over the 8254 chip. Enable interrupt 0 timer routing over the 8254 chip in addition to routing over the IO-APIC. The kernel tries to set a reasonable default, but sometimes this option is necessary to override it.

disable_8254_ timer	Disable interrupt 0 timer routing over the 8254 chip.
	Disable interrupt 0 timer routing over the 8254 chip in addition to routing over the IO-APIC. The kernel tries to set a reasonable default, but sometimes this option is necessary to override it.

hpet	Disable HPET and use PIT instead.
	`hpet=disable`
	Disable the HPET timer source and tell the kernel to use the PIT timer source instead.

clocksource	Set the specific clocksource.
	`clocksource=[hpet|pit|tsc|acpi_pm|cyclone|scx200_hrt]`
	Override the default kernel clocksource and use the clocksource with the specified name instead.

Miscellaneous Options

These options should always be available and don't depend on any specific subsystem or hardware being present in the system in order to work properly.

dhash_entries	Set the number of dentry hash buckets.
	`dhash_entries=n`
	This option lets you override the default number of hash buckets for the kernel's dentry cache. Recommended only for kernel experts.

elevator	Set the default I/O scheduler elevator.
	`elevator=[anticipatory|cfq|deadline|noop]`
	Specify the I/O scheduler. See Chapter 11 for a list of the different I/O schedulers available, and what they do.

hashdist	Distribute large hashes across NUMA nodes.
	`hashdist=[0|1]`
	Large hashes that are allocated during the boot process on the IA-64 platform are, by default, distributed across the different NUMA nodes. This option lets the user turn this option on or off.

combined_ mode	Specify IDE driver usage.

```
combined_mode=[combined|ide|libata]
```

Control which driver uses the IDE ports in combined mode: the legacy IDE driver, *libata*, or both. Note that using the ide or libata options may affect your device naming (e.g., by changing hdc to sdb).

max_loop	Maximum number of loopback devices.

```
max_loop=n
```

Specify the maximum number of loopback filesystem devices that can be mounted at the same time. *n* is an integer from 1 to 256.

panic	Time to wait after panic before rebooting.

```
panic=n
```

Specify the amount of time in seconds that the kernel should wait after a panic happens before it reboots. If this is set to 0 (the default value), the kernel will not reboot after panicking; it will simply halt.

pause_on_oops	Delay between kernel oopses.

```
pause_on_oops=n
```

Tell the kernel to halt all CPUs after the first oops for *n* seconds before continuing. This is useful if oopses keep scrolling off of the screen before you can write them down or take a picture of them.

profile	Control the kernel profiling.

```
profile=[schedule,][number]
```

This option affects how the kernel profiler is calculated. If schedule is specified, the schedule points are affected by the value set in *number*. If *schedule* is not specified, *number* is the step size as a power of two for statistical time-based profiling in the kernel.

The most common use of this option is profile=2.

10

Kernel Build Command-Line Reference

As discussed in Chapter 4, the tool that ties together kernel builds is the *make* program, to which you pass a target that specifies what you want to build. Chapter 4 went over the basic targets needed to build the kernel properly, but the kernel build system also has a wide range of other targets. This chapter details these targets, and what they can be used for.

All of these targets are passed to the *make* program on the command line, and a number of them can be grouped together if desired. For example:

```
$ make mrproper xconfig
```

The targets are broken down into different types in the following sections.

You can get a summary of most of these targets by running, within the build directory:

```
$ make help
```

This target prints out a lot of the common *make* targets that are described in the rest of this chapter.

Informational Targets

Table 10-1 shows targets that print the kernel version, based on a number of different options. They are commonly used by scripts to determine the version of the kernel being built.

Table 10-1. Informational targets

Target	Description
kernelrelease	Displays the current kernel version, as determined by the build system.
kernelversion	Displays the current kernel version, as told by the main *Makefile*. This differs from the kernelrelease target in that it doesn't use any additional version information based on configuration options or *localversion* files.

Cleaning Targets

Table 10-2 shows targets that simply remove files from previous builds. Their use is highly recommended to make sure you don't contaminate new builds with files leftover that may have been built with different options. They differ in how much they remove; sometimes you want to keep around files you've changed.

Table 10-2. Cleaning targets

Target	Description
clean	Removes most of the files generated by the kernel build system, but keeps the kernel configuration.
mrproper	Removes all of the generated files by the kernel build system, including the configuration and some various backup files.
distclean	Does everything mrproper does and removes some editor backup and patch leftover files.

Configuration Targets

Table 10-3 shows targets that allow the kernel to be configured in a wide range of different ways.

Table 10-3. Configuration targets

Target	Description
config	Updates the current kernel configuration by using a line-oriented program.
menuconfig	Updates the current kernel configuration by using a text-based menu program.
xconfig	Updates the current kernel configuration by using a QT-based graphical program.
gconfig	Updates the current kernel configuration by using a GTK+-based graphical program.
oldconfig	Updates the current kernel configuration by using the current *.config* file and prompting for any new options that have been added to the kernel.
silentoldconfig	Just like oldconfig, but prints nothing to the screen except when a question needs to be answered.
randconfig	Generates a new kernel configuration with random answers to all of the different options.
defconfig	Generates a new kernel configuration with the default answer being used for all options. The default values are taken from a file located in the *arch/$ARCH/defconfig* file, where *$ARCH* refers to the specific architecture for which the kernel is being built.
allmodconfig	Generates a new kernel configuration in which modules are enabled whenever possible.
allyesconfig	Generates a new kernel configuration with all options set to yes.
allnoconfig	Generates a new kernel configuration with all options set to no.

Note that the allyesconfig, allmodconfig, allnoconfig, and randconfig targets also take advantage of the environment variable KCONFIG_ALLCONFIG. If that variable points to a file, that file will be used as a list of configuration values that you require to be set to a specific value. In other words, the file overrides the normal behavior of the *make* targets.

For example, if the file *~/linux/must_be_set* contains the following variables:

```
$ cat ~/linux/must_be_set
CONFIG_SWAP=y
CONFIG_DEBUG_FS=y
```

and you enter *make allnoconfig* with the proper KCONFIG_ALLCONFIG environment variable in effect:

```
$ KCONFIG_ALLCONFIG=../must_be_set make allnoconfig
$ grep CONFIG_SWAP .config
CONFIG_SWAP=y
```

then the results include:

```
$ grep CONFIG_DEBUG_FS .config
CONFIG_DEBUG_FS=y
```

This variable would not have normally been set to y otherwise.

If the KCONFIG_ALLCONFIG variable is not set, the build system checks for files in the top-level build directory named:

- *allmod.config*
- *allno.config*
- *allrandom.config*
- *allyes.config*

If any of those files are present, the build uses them as lists of configuration values that must be forced to the specified values. If none of those files are found, the build system finally looks for a file called *all.config* for a list of forced configuration values.

You can use these different files to set up a known good base configuration that will always work. Then the other configuration options can be used to generate different testing configurations for the needed situation.

Build Targets

Table 10-4 shows targets that build the kernel itself in a variety of ways.

Table 10-4. Build targets

Target	Description
all	Builds all of the different targets needed for this kernel to be able to be used. This includes both the modules and the static portion of the kernel.
vmlinux	Builds just the static portion of the kernel, not any loadable modules.
modules	Builds all of the loadable kernel modules for this configuration.
modules_install	Installs all of the modules into the specified location. If no location is specified with the INSTALL_MODULE_PATH environment variable, they are installed in the default root directory of the machine.
dir/	Builds all of the files in the specified directory and in all subdirectories below it.
dir/file.[o|i|s]	Builds only the specified file.
dir/file.ko	Builds all of the needed files and links them together to form the specified module.
tags	Builds all of the needed tags that most common text editors can use while editing the source code.

Table 10-4. Build targets (continued)

Target	Description
TAGS	Builds all of the needed tags that most common text editors can use while editing the source code.
cscope	Builds a *cscope* image, useful in source tree searches, of the source tree for the architecture specified by the configuration file (not all of the kernel source files).

You can also pass a number of environment variables to *make* that will change the build. These can be specified for almost any target, as shown in Table 10-5.

Table 10-5. Environment variables

Variable	Value	Description
V	0	This tells the build system to run in a quiet manner, showing only the file that is currently being built, and not the entire command that is running in order to build that file. This is the default option for the build system.
V	1	This tells the build system to operate in a verbose way, showing the full command that is being used to generate each of the specific files.
O	dir	This tells the build system to locate all output files in the *dir* directory, including the kernel configuration files. This allows the kernel to be built from a read-only filesystem and have the output placed in another location.
C	1	This checks all C files that are about to be built with the *sparse* tool, which detects common programming errors in the kernel source files. *sparse* can be downloaded using *git* from *git://git.kernel.org/pub/scm/devel/sparse/sparse.git*. Nightly snapshots can be found at *http://www.codemonkey.org.uk/projects/git-snapshots/sparse/*. More information on how to use *sparse* can be found in the *Documentation/sparse.txt* file in the kernel source tree.
C	2	This forces all C files to be checked with the *sparse* tool, even if they did not need to be built.

Packaging Targets

These targets package up a built kernel into a standalone package that can be installed on a wide range of different machines, as shown in Table 10-6.

Table 10-6. Packaging targets

Target	Description
rpm	Builds the kernel first and then packages it up as a RPM package that can be installed.
rpm-pkg	Builds a source RPM package containing the base kernel.
binrpm-pkg	Builds a RPM package that contains a compiled kernel and modules.
deb-pkg	Builds a Debian package that contains the compiled kernel and modules.
tar-pkg	Builds a tarball that contains the compiled kernel and modules.
targz-pkg	Builds a *gzip*-compressed tarball that contains the compiled kernel and modules.
tarbz2-pkg	Builds a *bzip2*-compressed tarball that contains the compiled kernel and modules.

Documentation Targets

Table 10-7 shows targets that build the internal kernel documentation in a variety of different formats.

Table 10-7. Documentation targets

Target	Description
xmldocs	Builds the kernel documentation as XML DocBook files.
psdocs	Builds the kernel documentation as PostScript files.
pdfdocs	Builds the kernel documentation as PDF files.
htmldocs	Builds the kernel documentation as HTML files.
mandocs	Builds the kernel documentation as a set of manpages, which can then be installed with the *install-mandocs* target.

Architecture-Specific Targets

Each kernel architecture has a set of specific targets unique to it. Table 10-8 shows the targets available for the 32-bit Intel architecture.

Table 10-8. 32-bit Intel architecture-specific targets

Target	Description
bzImage	Creates a compressed kernel image and places it in the *arch/i386/boot/bzImage* file. This is the default target for the i386 kernel build.
install	Installs the kernel image using the distribution-specific */sbin/installkernel* program. Note that this does not install the kernel modules; that must be done with the *modules_install* target.
bzdisk	Creates a boot floppy image and writes it to the */dev/fd0* device.
fdimage	Creates a boot floppy image and places it in the file *arch/i386/boot/fdimage*. The *mtools* package must be present on your system in order for this to work properly.
isoimage	Creates a CD-ROM boot image and places it in the file *arch/i396/boot/image.iso*. The *syslinux* package must be present on your system in order for this to work properly.

Analysis Targets

Table 10-9 shows targets that are good for trying to find problem code in the kernel. It's a good idea to create a stack space list when creating new code to determine that your changes are not taking up too much kernel stack space. The namespacecheck target is useful for determining whether your changes can safely add its symbols to the kernel's global namespace.

Table 10-9. Analysis targets

Target	Description
checkstack	Generate a list of the functions that use the most of the kernel stack space.
namespacecheck	Generate a list of all of the kernel symbols and their namespaces. This will be a large list.

11

Kernel Configuration Option Reference

This chapter lists the most important configuration options offered when you run *make config* or one of its graphical interfaces. The majority of the chapter is based on the in-kernel documentation for the different kernel configuration options, which were written by the kernel developers and released under the GPL.

EXPERIMENTAL   Prompt for development and/or incomplete code/drivers

Some of the many things that Linux supports (such as network drivers, filesystems, network protocols, etc.) can be in a state of development where the functionality, stability, or the level of testing is not yet high enough for general use. This is usually known as the "alpha-test" phase among developers. If a feature is currently in alpha-test, the developers usually discourage uninformed widespread use of this feature by the general public to avoid "Why doesn't this work?" mail messages. However, active testing and use of these systems is welcomed. Just be aware that it may not meet the normal level of reliability or may fail to work in some special cases. Detailed bug reports from people familiar with the kernel internals are usually welcomed by the developers. (But before submitting bug reports, please read the documents README, MAINTAINERS, REPORTING-BUGS, *Documentation/ BUG-HUNTING*, and *Documentation/oops-tracing.txt* in the kernel source.)

This option also makes obsolete drivers available. These are drivers that have been replaced by something else and/or are scheduled to be removed in a future kernel release.

Unless you intend to help test and develop a feature or driver that falls into this category, or you have a situation that requires using these features, you should probably say no here, which will cause the configurator to present you with fewer choices. If you say yes here, you will be offered the choice of using features or drivers that are currently considered to be in the alpha-test phase.

On its own, this option does not do anything except allow you to select other options.

Configuration
Reference

LOCALVERSION — Local version—append to kernel release

This allows you to append an extra string to the end of your kernel version. This will show up when you enter a *uname* command, for example. The string you set here will be appended after the contents of any files with a filename beginning with *localversion* in your object and source tree, in that order. The string can be a maximum of 64 characters.

AUDIT — Auditing support

Enable an auditing infrastructure that can be used with another kernel subsystem, such as SELinux (which requires this for logging of avc messages output).

IKCONFIG — Kernel *.config* support

This option enables the complete Linux kernel *.config* file contents to be saved in the kernel. It documents which kernel options are used in a running kernel or an on-disk kernel. This information can be extracted from the kernel image file with the script *scripts/extract-ikconfig* and used as input to rebuild the current kernel or to build another kernel. It can also be extracted from a running kernel by reading the file */proc/config.gz*.

EMBEDDED — Configure standard kernel features (for small systems)

This option allows certain base kernel options and settings to be disabled or tweaked. This is for specialized environments that can tolerate a "nonstandard" kernel. This is recommend only for experts, as it is very easy to change the options to create a kernel that will not even boot properly.

On its own, this option does not do anything except allow you to select other options.

MODULES — Enable loadable module support

Kernel modules are small pieces of compiled code that can be inserted in the running kernel, rather than being permanently built into the kernel. If you select this option, many parts of the kernel can be built as modules (by answering M instead of yes where indicated): this is most useful for infrequently used options that are not required for booting. For more information, see Chapter 4 and the manpages for *modprobe, lsmod, modinfo, insmod,* and *rmmod.*

If you say yes here, you will need to run *make modules_install* to put the modules under */lib/modules* where the module tools can find them.

IOSCHED_NOOP	No-op I/O scheduler

The no-op I/O scheduler is a minimal scheduler that does basic merging and sorting. Its main uses include nondisk-based block devices such as memory devices and specialized software or hardware environments that do their own scheduling and require only minimal assistance from the kernel.

IOSCHED_AS	Anticipatory I/O scheduler

The anticipatory I/O scheduler is the default disk scheduler. It is generally a good choice for most environments, but is quite large and complex compared to the deadline I/O scheduler. It can also be slower in some cases, especially under some database loads.

IOSCHED_ DEADLINE	Deadline I/O scheduler

The deadline I/O scheduler is simple and compact. It is often as good as the anticipatory I/O scheduler, and under some database workloads, even better. In the case of a single process performing I/O to a disk at any one time, its behavior is almost identical to the anticipatory I/O scheduler and so is a good choice.

IOSCHED_CFQ	CFQ I/O scheduler

The CFQ I/O scheduler tries to distribute bandwidth equally among all processes in the system. It should provide a fair working environment, suitable for desktop systems.

SMP	Symmetric multiprocessing support

This enables support for systems with more than one CPU. If you have a system with only one CPU, like most personal computers, say no. If you have a system with more than one CPU, say yes.

If you say no here, the kernel will run on single and multiprocessor machines, but will use only one CPU of a multiprocessor machine. If you say yes here, the kernel will run on many, but not all, single-processor machines. On a single-processor machine, the kernel will run faster if you say no here.

Note that if you say yes here and choose architecture 586 or Pentium under Processor family, the kernel will not work on 486 architectures. Similarly, multiprocessor kernels for the PPro architecture may not work on all Pentium-based boards.

See also *Documentation/smp.txt, Documentation/i386/IO-APIC.txt, Documentation/nmi_watchdog.txt*, and the SMP-HOWTO available at *http://www.tldp.org/docs.html#howto*.

This is the processor type of your CPU. This information is used for optimization. In order to compile a kernel that can run on all x86 CPU types (albeit not optimally fast), you can specify 386 here.

The kernel will not necessarily run on earlier architectures than the one you have chosen; e.g., a Pentium-optimized kernel will run on a PPro, but not necessarily on a i486.

Here are the settings recommended for greatest speed:

386
> Choose this if you have an AMD/Cyrix/Intel 386DX/DXL/SL/ SLC/SX, Cyrix/TI 486DLC/DLC2, UMC 486SX-S, or NexGen Nx586 processor. Only 386 kernels will run on a 386 class machine.

486
> Choose this if you have an AMD/Cyrix/IBM/Intel 486DX/ DX2/DX4, SL/SLC/SLC2/SLC3/SX/SX2 and UMC U5D, or U5S processor.

586
> Choose this if you have a generic Pentium processor lacking the TSC (timestamp counter) register.

Pentium-Classic
> Choose this if you have an Intel Pentium processor.

Pentium-MMX
> Choose this if you have an Intel Pentium MMX processor.

Pentium-Pro
> Choose this if you have an Intel Pentium Pro processor.

Pentium-II
> Choose this if you have an Intel Pentium II or pre-Coppermine Celeron processor.

Pentium-III
> Choose this if you have an Intel Pentium III or Coppermine Celeron processor.

Pentium-4
> Choose this if you have an Intel Pentium 4 or P4-based Celeron processor.

K6
> Choose this if you have an AMD K6, K6-II or K6-III (aka K6-3D) processor.

Athlon
> Choose this if you have an AMD K7 family (Athlon/Duron/ Thunderbird) processor.

Crusoe
> Choose this if you have a Transmeta Crusoe series processor.

Efficeon
> Choose this if you have a Transmeta Efficeon series processor.

Winchip-C6
> Choose this if you have an original IDT Winchip processor.

Winchip-2
> Choose this if you have an IDT Winchip 2 processor.

Winchip-2
> Choose this if you have an IDT Winchip processor with 3DNow! capabilities.

GeodeGX1
> Choose this if you have a Geode GX1 (Cyrix MediaGX) processor.

Geode GX/LX
> Choose this if you have an AMD Geode GX or LX processor.

CyrixIII/VIA C3
> Choose this if you have a VIA Cyrix III or VIA C3 processor.

VIA C3-2
> Choose this if you have a VIA C3-2 "Nehemiah" (model 9 and above) processor.

If you don't know what to do, choose 386.

X86_GENERIC

Generic x86 support

Instead of just including optimizations for the selected x86 variant (e.g., PII, Crusoe, or Athlon), include some more generic optimizations as well. This will make the kernel perform better on x86 CPUs other than the one selected.

This is really intended for distributors who need more generic optimizations.

NR_CPUS

Maximum number of CPUs (2-255)

This allows you to specify the maximum number of CPUs that this kernel will support. The maximum supported value is 255 and the minimum value that makes sense is 2.

This option is purely to save memory; each supported CPU adds approximately 8 KB to the kernel image.

SCHED_SMT

SMT (HyperThreading) scheduler support

SMT scheduler support improves the CPU scheduler's decision-making on Intel Pentium 4 chips with HyperThreading, at a cost of slightly increased overhead in some places.

PREEMPT_NONE No forced preemption (server)

This is the traditional Linux preemption model, geared toward maximizing throughput. It still provides good latency most of the time, occasional longer delays are possible.

Select this option if you are building a kernel for a server or scientific/computation system, or if you want to maximize the raw processing power of the kernel, irrespective of scheduling latencies.

PREEMPT_ VOLUNTARY Voluntary kernel preemption (desktop)

This option reduces the latency of the kernel by adding more "explicit preemption points" to the kernel code. These new preemption points have been selected to reduce the maximum latency of rescheduling, which provides faster response to applications at the cost of slighly lower throughput.

This option speeds up reaction to interactive events by allowing a low-priority process to voluntarily preempt itself even if it is in kernel mode executing a system call. This allows applications to appear to run more smoothly even when the system is under load.

Select this if you are building a kernel for a desktop system.

PREEMPT Preemptible kernel (low-latency desktop)

This option reduces the latency of the kernel by making all kernel code (except code executing in a critical section) preemptible. This allows reaction to interactive events by permitting a low priority process to be preempted involuntarily even if the processor is in kernel mode executing a system call and would otherwise not be about to reach a natural preemption point. This allows applications to appear to run more smoothly even when the system is under load, at the cost of slighly lower throughput and a slight runtime overhead to kernel code.

Select this if you are building a kernel for a desktop or an embedded system with latency requirements in the milliseconds range.

PREEMPT_BKL Preempt the Big Kernel Lock

This option reduces the latency of the kernel by making the Big Kernel Lock preemptible.

Say yes here if you are building a kernel for a desktop system.

NOHIGHMEM High memory configuration

Linux can use up to 64 GB of physical memory on x86 systems. However, the address space of 32-bit x86 processors is only 4 GB in size. That means that, if you have a large amount of physical memory, not all of it can be permanently mapped by the kernel. The physical memory that's not permanently mapped is called *high memory*.

If you are compiling a kernel that will never run on a machine with more than 1 GB total physical RAM, answer off here (the default choice, and suitable for most users). This will result in a 3 GB/1 GB split: 3 GB are mapped so that each process sees a 3 GB virtual memory space and the remaining part of the 4 GB virtual memory space is used by the kernel to permanently map as much physical memory as possible.

If the machine has between 1 and 4 GB physical RAM, answer 4GB here.

If more than 4 GB is used, answer 64GB here. This selection turns Intel PAE (Physical Address Extension) mode on. PAE implements three-level paging on IA32 processors. PAE is fully supported by Linux, and PAE mode is implemented on all recent Intel processors (Pentium Pro and better).

 If you say 64GB here, the kernel will not boot on CPUs that don't support PAE!

The actual amount of total physical memory will either be autodetected or can be forced by using a kernel command line option such as mem=256M. (See Chapter 9 for details about how to pass options to the kernel at boot time, and what options are available.)

If unsure, say off.

HIGHMEM4G   4GB

Select this if you have a 32-bit processor and between 1 and 4 GB of physical RAM.

HIGHMEM64G   64GB

Select this if you have a 32-bit processor and more than 4 GB of physical RAM.

FLATMEM_   Flat memory
MANUAL

This option allows you to change some of the ways that Linux manages its memory internally. Most users will see only have one option here: FLATMEM. This is normal and a correct option.

Some users of more advanced features, such as NUMA and memory hotplug, may have different options here. DISCONTIGMEM is a more mature, better tested system, but is incompatible with memory hotplug and may suffer decreased performance over SPARSEMEM. If you are unsure between sparse memory and discontiguous memory, choose discontiguous memory.

If unsure, choose this option, flat memory.

DISCONTIGMEM _MANUAL

Discontiguous memory

This option provides better support than flat memory for discontiguous memory systems. These systems have holes in their physical address spaces, and this option handles the holes more efficiently. However, the vast majority of hardware has quite flat address spaces and can experience degraded performance from the extra overhead this option imposes.

Many NUMA configurations will have this as the only option.

If unsure, choose flat memory over this option.

SPARSEMEM_ MANUAL

Sparse memory

This will be the only option for some systems, including memory hotplug systems.

For many other systems, this will be an alternative to discontiguous memory. This option provides some potential performance benefits, along with decreased code complexity, but it is newer and more experimental.

If you are unsure, choose discontiguous memory or flat memory.

SECCOMP

Enable seccomp to safely compute untrusted bytecode

This kernel feature is useful for number-crunching applications that may need to compute untrusted bytecode during their execution. By using pipes or other transports made available to the process as file descriptors supporting the read/write syscalls, it's possible to isolate those applications in their own address space using seccomp. Once seccomp is enabled via /proc/pid/seccomp, it cannot be disabled and the task is allowed to execute only a few safe syscalls defined by each seccomp mode.

If you are unsure, say yes. Only embedded systems should be built by answering no.

KEXEC

kexec system call (experimental)

kexec is a system call that implements the ability to shut down your current kernel and start up another. It is like a reboot, but is independent of the system firmware. And like a reboot, you can start any kernel with it, not just Linux.

The name comes from the similarity to the exec system call.

Do not be surprised if this code does not initially work for you. It may help to enable device hotplugging support. As of this writing, the exact hardware interface is strongly in flux, so no good recommendation can be made.

HOTPLUG_CPU   Support for hot-pluggable CPUs (experimental)

Say yes here to experiment with turning CPUs off and on, and to enable suspend on SMP systems. CPUs can be controlled through the */sys/devices/system/cpu* interface.

PM   Power management support

Power management allows parts of your computer to shut off or be put into a power-conserving sleep mode if they are not being used. There are two competing standards for doing this: APM and ACPI. If you want to use either one, say yes here and then also enable one of those two standards.

Power management is most important for battery-powered laptop computers; if you have a laptop, check out the Linux Laptop home page at *http://www.linux-on-laptops.com*, Tuxmobil-Linux on Mobile Computers at *http://www.tuxmobil.org*, and the "Battery Powered Linux" mini-HOWTO at *http://www.tldp.org/docs.html#howto*.

Note that, even if you say no here, Linux on the x86 architecture will issue the HLT instruction if nothing is being done, thereby sending the processor to sleep and saving power.

SOFTWARE_   Software suspend
SUSPEND
                    Enable machine suspension.

When the machine is suspended, an image is saved in your active swap. Upon next boot, pass the resume=*/dev/swappartition* argument to the kernel to have it detect the saved image, restore memory state from it, and continue to run as before. If you do not want the previous state to be reloaded, use the noresume kernel argument. However, note that your partitions will be *fsck*'d and you must issue *mkswap* on your swap partitions again. The procedure does not work with swap files.

Right now you may boot without resuming and then resume later, but in the meantime you cannot use those swap partitions/files that were involved in suspending. In this case, also, there is a risk that buffers on disk won't match with saved ones.

For more information, see *Documentation/power/swsusp.txt*.

ACPI   ACPI Support

Advanced Configuration and Power Interface (ACPI) support for Linux requires ACPI-compliant hardware and firmware, and assumes the presence of OS-directed configuration and power

---

management (OSPM) software. This option will enlarge your kernel by about 70 KB.

Linux ACPI provides a robust functional replacement for several legacy configuration and power management interfaces, including the Plug and Play BIOS specification (PnP BIOS), the MultiProcessor specification (MPS), and the Advanced Power Management (APM) specification. If both ACPI and APM support are configured, whichever is loaded first will be used.

The ACPI SourceForge project at *http://sourceforge.net/projects/acpi* contains the latest source code, documentation, tools, mailing list subscription, and other information.

Linux support for ACPI is based on Intel Corporation's ACPI Component Architecture (ACPI CA). For more information, see *http://developer.intel.com/technology/iapc/acpi*.

ACPI is an open industry specification codeveloped by Compaq, Intel, Microsoft, Phoenix, and Toshiba. The specification is available at *http://www.acpi.info*.

CPU_FREQ	CPU frequency scaling

CPU frequency scaling allows you to change the clock speed of CPUs on the fly. This can save power, because the lower the CPU clock speed, the less power the CPU consumes.

Note that this driver doesn't automatically change the CPU clock speed; you need to either enable a dynamic CPUFreq policy governor (described later) after booting or use a userspace tool.

For details, take a look at *Documentation/cpu-freq*.

CPU_FREQ_ DEFAULT_GOV_ PERFORMANCE	Performance

Use the CPUFreq performance governor. This sets the frequency statically to the highest frequency supported by the CPU.

CPU_FREQ_ DEFAULT_GOV_ USERSPACE	Userspace

Use the CPUFreq userspace governor. This allows you to set the CPU frequency manually and allows a userspace program to set the CPU dynamically without requiring you to first enable the userspace governor manually.

CPU_FREQ_ GOV_ PERFORMANCE	"Performance" CPUFreq policy governor

This CPUFreq policy governor sets the frequency statically to the highest available CPU frequency.

CPU_FREQ_ GOV_ POWERSAVE	"Powersave" CPUFreq policy governor
	This sets the frequency statically to the lowest available CPU frequency.

CPU_FREQ_ GOV_ USERSPACE	"Userspace" CPUFreq policy governor
	Enable this CPUFreq policy governor either when you want to set the CPU frequency manually or when a userspace program should be able to set the CPU dynamically, as on LART (*http://www.lart-maker.nl*).
	For details, take a look at *Documentation/cpu-freq.*

CPU_FREQ_ GOV_ ONDEMAND	"Ondemand" CPUFreq policy governor
	This driver adds a dynamic CPUFreq policy governor. The governor polls the CPU and changes its frequency based on CPU utilization. Support for this governor depends on the CPU's ability to do fast frequency switching (i.e., very low latency frequency transitions).
	For details, take a look at *Documentation/cpu-freq.*

CPU_FREQ_ GOV_ CONSERVATIVE	"Conservative" CPUFreq policy governor
	This driver is similar to the Ondemand governor both in its source code and its purpose. The difference is that the Conservative governor is optimized for a battery-powered system. The frequency is gracefully increased and decreased rather than jumping to 100 percent when speed is required.
	If you are using a laptop, a PDA, or an AMD64-based computer (due to the unacceptable step-by-step latency issues between the minimum and maximum frequency transitions in the CPU), you will probably want to use this governor. If you have a desktop machine, consider the Ondemand governor instead.
	For details, take a look at *Documentation/cpu-freq.*

PCI	PCI support
	PCI is a bus system used by the processor to talk to internal devices and add-on cards. It is extremely common and found in almost all modern computers.
	Say yes to this option unless you have a special reason not to.

PCCARD	PCCard (PCMCIA/CardBus) support
	Say yes here if you want to attach PCMCIA or PC cards to your Linux computer. These are credit-card size devices such as network cards, modems, or hard drives often used with laptop computers.

There are actually two varieties of these cards: 16-bit PCMCIA and 32-bit CardBus cards.

PCMCIA   16-bit PCMCIA support

This option enables support for 16-bit PCMCIA cards. Most older PC cards are 16-bit PCMCIA cards, so unless you know you're only using 32-bit CardBus cards, say yes here.

To use 16-bit PCMCIA cards, you will need supporting software in most cases. See the file *Documentation/Changes* for location and details.

CARDBUS   32-bit CardBus support

CardBus is a bus mastering architecture for PC cards, which allows for 32-bit PC cards (the original PCMCIA standard specifies only a 16-bit wide bus). Many newer PC cards are actually CardBus cards.

To use 32-bit PC cards, you also need a CardBus-compatible host bridge. Virtually all modern PCMCIA bridges do this, and most of them are "yenta-compatible," so enable that option too.

HOTPLUG_PCI   Support for PCI hotplug (experimental)

Say yes here if you have a motherboard with a PCI hotplug controller. This allows you to add and remove PCI cards while the machine is powered up and running.

NET   Networking support

Say yes here unless you are an expert with a really good reason not to. The reason is that some programs need kernel networking support even when running on a standalone machine that isn't connected to any other computer.

If you are upgrading from an older kernel, you should consider updating your networking tools too, because changes in the kernel and the tools often go hand in hand. The tools are contained in the *net-tools* package, the location and version number of which are given in *Documentation/Changes*.

For a general introduction to Linux networking, it is highly recommended that you read the NET-HOWTO, available from *http://www.tldp.org/docs.html#howto*.

UNIX   Unix domain sockets

If you say yes here, you will include support for Unix domain sockets; sockets are the standard Unix mechanism for establishing and accessing network connections. Many commonly used programs such as the X Window System, *syslog*, and *udev* use these sockets even if your machine is not connected to any network. Unless you are working on an embedded system or something similar, you definitely want to say yes here.

INET TCP/IP networking

These are the protocols used on the Internet and on most local Ethernets. It is highly recommended that you say yes here, since some programs (e.g., the X Window System) use TCP/IP even if your machine is not connected to any other computer. They use the so-called *loopback device*, which this option sets up. It will enlarge your kernel by about 144 KB.

For an excellent introduction to Linux networking, please read the "Linux Networking" HOWTO, available from *http://www.tldp.org/docs.html#howto*.

IP_ADVANCED_ IP: advanced router
ROUTER

If you intend to run your Linux box mostly as a router, i.e., as a computer that forwards and redistributes network packets, say yes here. You will then be presented with several options that allow more precise control about the routing process.

The answer to this question won't directly affect the kernel: answering no will just cause the configurator to skip all the questions about advanced routing.

Note that your box can act as a router only if you enable IP forwarding in your kernel; you can do that by saying yes to the */proc* filesystem support and Sysctl support options and executing the line:

```
echo "1" > /proc/sys/net/ipv4/ip_forward
```

at boot time after the */proc* filesystem has been mounted.

If you turn on IP forwarding, you will also get rp_filter, which automatically rejects incoming packets if the routing table entry for their source address doesn't match the network interface they're arriving on. This has security advantages because it prevents IP spoofing; however, it can pose problems if you use asymmetric routing (packets from you to a host take a different path from packets that go from that host to you) or if you operate a nonrouting host that has several IP addresses on different interfaces. To turn rp_filter off, enter:

```
echo 0 > /proc/sys/net/ipv4/conf/device/rp_filter
```

or:

```
echo 0 > /proc/sys/net/ipv4/conf/all/rp_filter
```

NETFILTER Network packet filtering

Netfilter is a framework for filtering and mangling network packets that pass through your Linux box.

The most common use of packet filtering is to run your Linux box as a firewall protecting a local network from the Internet. The type of firewall provided by this kernel support is called a *packet filter*, which means that it can reject individual network packets based on type, source, destination, etc. The other kind of firewall, a *proxy-based* one, is more secure but more intrusive and more bothersome to set up; it inspects the network traffic much more closely, modifies it, and has knowledge about the higher-level protocols, which a packet filter lacks. Moreover, proxy-based firewalls often require changes to the programs running on the local clients. Proxy-based firewalls don't need support by the kernel, but they are often combined with a packet filter, which works only if you say yes here.

You should also say yes here if you intend to use your Linux box as the gateway to the Internet for a local network of machines without globally valid IP addresses. This is called *masquerading*. If one of the computers on your local network wants to send something to the outside, your box can "masquerade" as that computer, i.e., it forwards the traffic to the intended outside destination, but modifies the packets to make it look like they came from the firewall box itself. Masquerading works both ways: if the outside host replies, the Linux box will silently forward the traffic to the correct local computer. This way, the computers on your local net are completely invisible to the outside world, even though they can reach the outside and can receive replies. It is even possible to run globally visible servers from within a masqueraded local network using a mechanism called port forwarding. Masquerading is also often called NAT (Network Address Translation). Other operating systems often call this term PAT (Port Address Translation).

Another use of Netfilter is in transparent proxying: if a machine on the local network tries to connect to an outside host, your Linux box can transparently forward the traffic to a local server, typically a caching proxy server.

Yet another use of Netfilter is building a bridging firewall. Using a bridge with Network packet filtering enabled makes iptables "see" the bridged traffic. For filtering on the lower network and Ethernet protocols over the bridge, use ebtables (located under bridge Netfilter configuration).

Various modules exist for Netfilter that replace the previous masquerading (*ipmasqadm*), packet-filtering (*ipchains*), transparent proxying, and port-forwarding mechanisms. Please see *Documentation/Changes* under *iptables* for the location of these packages.

Chances are that you should say yes here if you compile a kernel which will run as a router and no for regular hosts.

NET_SCHED   QoS and/or fair queueing

When the kernel has several packets to send out over a network device, it has to decide which ones to send first, which ones to delay, and which ones to drop. This is the job of queueing disciplines. Several different algorithms for how to do this "fairly" have been proposed.

If you say no here, you will get the standard packet scheduler, which is a FIFO (first come, first served) scheduler. If you say yes here, you will be able to choose from among several alternative algorithms that can then be attached to different network devices. This is useful, for example, if some of your network devices are real-time devices that need a certain minimum data flow rate, or if you need to limit the maximum data flow rate for traffic that matches specified criteria.

To administer these schedulers, you'll need the user-level utilities from the package *iproute2+tc* at *http://linux-net.osdl.org/index.php/ Iproute2*.

This Quality of Service (QoS) support will enable you to use Differentiated Services (diffserv) and Resource Reservation Protocol (RSVP) on your Linux router if you also say yes to the corresponding options. Documentation and software is at *http://diffserv. sourceforge.net*.

IRDA   IrDA (infrared) subsystem support

Say yes here if you want to build support for the IrDA protocols. The Infrared Data Association specifies standards for wireless infrared communication and is supported by most laptops and PDAs.

To use Linux support for the IrDA protocols, you will also need some userspace utilities such as *irattach*. For more information, see the file *Documentation/networking/irda.txt*. You also want to read the IR-HOWTO, available at *http://www.tldp.org/docs.html#howto*.

If you want to exchange bits of data (e.g., vCal, vCard) with a PDA, you will need to install an OBEX application, such as OpenObex from *http://sourceforge.net/projects/openobex*.

IRLAN   IrLAN protocol

Say yes here if you want to build support for the IrLAN protocol. IrLAN emulates an Ethernet and makes it possible to put up a wireless LAN using infrared beams.

The IrLAN protocol can be used to talk with infrared access points such as the HP NetbeamIR or the ESI JetEye NET. You can also connect to another Linux machine running the IrLAN protocol for ad hoc networking.

IRNET   IrNET protocol

Say yes here if you want to build support for the IrNET protocol. IrNET is a PPP driver, so you will also need a working PPP subsystem (driver, daemon, and configuration).

IrNET is an alternate way to transfer TCP/IP traffic over IrDA. It uses synchronous PPP over a set of point to point IrDA sockets. You can use it between Linux machines or with Windows.

IRCOMM   IrCOMM protocol

Say yes here if you want to build support for the IrCOMM protocol. IrCOMM implements serial port emulation, and makes it possible to use all existing applications that understand ttys with infrared links. Thus, you should be able to use applications such as PPP and *minicom*.

IRDA_ULTRA   Ultra (connectionless) protocol

Say yes here to support the connectionless Ultra IRDA protocol. Ultra allows you to exchange data over IrDA with really simple devices (watch, beacon) without the overhead of the IrDA protocol (no handshaking, no management frames, simple fixed header). Ultra is available as a special socket: socket(AF_IRDA, SOCK_DGRAM, 1).

BT   Bluetooth subsystem support

Bluetooth is a low-cost, low-power, and short-range wireless technology. It was designed as a replacement for cables and other short-range technologies such as IrDA. Bluetooth operates in a personal area range that typically extends up to 10 meters. More information about Bluetooth can be found at *http://www.bluetooth.com*.

The Linux Bluetooth subsystem consist of several layers:

Bluetooth core
   HCI device and connection manager, scheduler

HCI device drivers
   Interface to the hardware

SCO module
   SCO audio links

L2CAP module
   Logical Link Control and Adaptation Protocol

RFCOMM module
   RFCOMM Protocol

BNEP
   Module Bluetooth Network Encapsulation Protocol

CMTP
   Module CAPI Message Transport Protocol

HIDP

Module Human Interface Device Protocol

To use the Linux Bluetooth subsystem, you will need several user-space utilities, such as *hciconfig* and *hcid*. These utilities and updates to Bluetooth kernel modules are provided in the BlueZ packages at *http://www.bluez.org*.

IEEE80211   Generic IEEE 802.11 networking stack

This option enables the hardware-independent IEEE 802.11 networking stack.

MTD   Memory Technology Device (MTD) support

Memory Technology Devices are flash, RAM, and similar chips, often used for solid-state filesystems on embedded devices. This option provides the generic support for MTD drivers to register themselves with the kernel and for potential users of MTD devices to enumerate the devices present and obtain a handle on them. It also allows you to select individual drivers for particular hardware and users of MTD devices.

PARPORT   Parallel port support

If you want to use devices connected to your machine's parallel port (the connector at the computer with 25 holes), e.g., a printer, ZIP drive, or Parallel Line Internet Protocol (PLIP) link, you need to say yes here.

Please read *Documentation/parport.txt* and *drivers/parport/BUGS-parport* for more information. For extensive information about drivers for many devices attaching to the parallel port, see *http://www.torque.net/linux-pp.html*.

It is possible to share a single parallel port among several devices, and it is safe to compile all the corresponding drivers into the kernel. If you have more than one parallel port and want to specify which port and IRQ will be used by this driver at module load time, take a look at *Documentation/parport.txt*.

PNP   Plug and Play support

Plug and Play (PnP) is a standard for peripherals that allows them to be configured by software—for example, to assign IRQs or other parameters. No jumpers on the cards are needed; instead, the values are provided to the cards from the BIOS, from the operating system, or using a userspace utility.

Say yes here if you would like Linux to configure your PnP devices. You should then also say yes to all of the protocols needed. Alternatively, you can say no here and configure your PnP devices using userspace utilities such as the *isapnptools* package.

ISAPNP   ISA Plug and Play support

Say yes here if you would like support for ISA PnP devices. Some information is available in *Documentation/isapnp.txt*.

If you use have ISA Plug and Play devices, please use the ISA PnP tools found at *http://www.roestock.demon.co.uk/isapnptools* to configure them properly.

PNPBIOS   Plug and Play BIOS support (experimental)

Linux uses the PNPBIOS defined in "Plug and Play BIOS Specification Version 1.0A May 5, 1994" to autodetect built-in mainboard resources (e.g., parallel port resources).

If you would like the kernel to detect and allocate resources to your mainboard devices (on some systems they are disabled by the BIOS) say yes here. The PNPBIOS can also help prevent resource conflicts between mainboard devices and other bus devices.

ACPI is expected to supersede PNPBIOS some day. Currently, they coexist nicely. If you have a non-ISA system that supports ACPI, you probably don't need PNPBIOS support.

IDE   ATA/ATAPI/MFM/RLL support

If you say yes here, your kernel will be able to manage low-cost mass storage units such as ATA/(E)IDE and ATAPI. The most common examples of such devices are IDE hard drives and ATAPI CD-ROM drives.

If your system is pure SCSI and doesn't use these interfaces, you can say no here.

- Integrated Disk Electronics (IDE, also known as ATA-1) is a connecting standard for mass storage units such as hard disks. It was designed by Western Digital and Compaq Computer in 1984. It was then named ST506. Several disks use the IDE interface.

- AT Attachment (ATA) is the superset of the IDE specifications. ST506 is also called ATA-1.

- Fast-IDE is ATA-2 (also named Fast ATA).

- Enhanced IDE (EIDE) is ATA-3. It provides support for larger disks (up to 8.4 GB by means of the LBA standard), more disks (four instead of two), and for other mass storage units, such as tapes and CD-ROMs.

- UDMA/33 (also known as UltraDMA/33) is ATA-4. By using fast DMA controllers, it provides faster transfer modes (with less load on the CPU) than previous PIO (Programmed processor Input/Output) from previous ATA/IDE standards.

- ATA Packet Interface (ATAPI) is a protocol used by EIDE tape and CD-ROM drives, similar in many respects to the SCSI protocol.

SMART IDE (self-monitoring, -analysis, and -reporting technology) was designed in order to prevent data corruption and disk crashes by detecting pre-hardware failure conditions (heat, access time, and the like). Disks built after June 1995 may follow this standard. The kernel itself doesn't manage this; however, there are quite a number of user programs, such as *smart*, that can query the status of SMART parameters from disk drives.

For further information, please read *Documentation/ide.txt*.

BLK_DEV_IDE   Enhanced IDE/MFM/RLL disk/CD-ROM/tape/floppy support

If you say yes here, you will use the full-featured IDE driver to control up to 10 ATA/IDE interfaces, each one able to serve a "master" and a "slave" device, for a total of up to 20 ATA/IDE disk/CD-ROM/tape/floppy drives.

Useful information about large (540 MB) IDE disks, multiple interfaces, what to do if ATA/IDE devices are not automatically detected, sound card ATA/IDE ports, module support, and other topics is contained in *Documentation/ide.txt*. For detailed information about hard drives, consult the Disk-HOWTO and the Multi-Disk-HOWTO, available at *http://www.tldp.org/docs.html#howto*.

To fine-tune ATA/IDE drive/interface parameters for improved performance, look for the *hdparm* package at *ftp://ibiblio.org/pub/Linux/system/hardware*.

Do not compile this driver as a module if your root filesystem (the one containing the directory /) is located on an IDE device.

If you have one or more IDE drives, enable this option. If your system has no IDE drives or if memory requirements are really tight, you could say no here, and select the old hard disk driver option instead to save about 13 KB of memory in the kernel.

BLK_DEV_   Include IDE/ATA-2 disk support
IDEDISK
This includes enhanced support for MFM/RLL/IDE hard disks. If you have a MFM/RLL/IDE disk and there is no special reason to use the old hard disk driver instead, say yes. If you have an SCSI-only system, you can say no here.

Do not compile this driver as a module if your root filesystem (the one containing the directory /) is located on the IDE disk.

BLK_DEV_   Include IDE/ATAPI CD-ROM support
IDECD
If you have a CD-ROM drive using the ATAPI protocol, say yes here. ATAPI is a newer protocol used by IDE CD-ROM and tape drives, similar to the SCSI protocol. Most new CD-ROM drives use ATAPI, including the NEC-260, Mitsumi FX400, Sony 55E, and just about all non-SCSI double (2×) or better speed drives.

If you say yes here, the CD-ROM drive will be identified at boot time along with other IDE devices, as something such as hdb or hdc (check the boot messages using the *dmesg* command). If this is your only CD-ROM drive, you can say no to all other CD-ROM options, but be sure to also enable the ISO 9660 CD-ROM filesystem support option.

Note that older versions of LILO (LInux LOader) cannot properly deal with IDE/ATAPI CD-ROMs, so install LILO 16 or higher, available from *http://lilo.go.dyndns.org*.

BLK_DEV_ IDEFLOPPY

Include IDE/ATAPI floppy support

If you have an IDE floppy drive that uses the ATAPI protocol, answer yes. ATAPI is a newer protocol used by IDE CD-ROM/ tape/floppy drives, similar to the SCSI protocol.

The LS-120 and the IDE/ATAPI Iomega ZIP drive are also supported by this driver. For information about jumper settings and the question of when a ZIP drive uses a partition table, see *http://www.win.tue.nl/~aeb/linux/zip/zip-1.html*. (ATAPI PD-CD/ CDR drives are not supported by this driver; support for PD-CD/ CDR drives is available if you answer yes to SCSI emulation support).

If you say yes here, the floppy drive will be identified along with other IDE devices, with a name such as hdb or hdc (check the boot messages using the *dmesg* command).

SCSI

SCSI device support

If you want to use a SCSI hard disk, SCSI tape drive, SCSI CD-ROM, or any other SCSI device under Linux, say yes and make sure that you know the name of your SCSI host adapter (the card inside your computer that "speaks" the SCSI protocol, also called SCSI controller), because you will be asked for it.

You also need to say yes here if you have a device that speaks the SCSI protocol. Examples of these include the parallel port version of the IOMEGA ZIP drive, USB storage devices, Fibre Channel, FireWire storage, and the IDE-SCSI emulation driver.

Do not compile this as a module if your root filesystem (the one containing the directory /) is located on a SCSI device.

BLK_DEV_SD

SCSI disk support

If you want to use SCSI hard disks, Fibre Channel disks, USB storage, or the SCSI or parallel port version of the IOMEGA ZIP drive, say yes and read the SCSI-HOWTO, the Disk-HOWTO, and the Multi-Disk-HOWTO, available from *http://www.tldp.org/docs. html#howto*. This is *not* for SCSI CD-ROMs.

Do not compile this driver as a module if your root filesystem (the one containing the directory /) is located on a SCSI disk. In this case, do not compile the driver for your SCSI host adapter as a module either.

CHR_DEV_ST SCSI tape support

If you want to use a SCSI tape drive under Linux, say yes and read the SCSI-HOWTO, available from *http://www.tldp.org/docs. html#howto*, and *Documentation/scsi/st.txt* in the kernel source. This is *not* for SCSI CD-ROMs.

BLK_DEV_SR SCSI CD-ROM support

If you want to use a SCSI or FireWire CD-ROM under Linux, say yes and read the SCSI-HOWTO and the CDROM-HOWTO at *http://www.tldp.org/docs.html#howto* for more directions. Also make sure to enable the ISO 9660 CD-ROM filesystem support option.

CHR_DEV_SG SCSI generic support

If you want to use SCSI scanners, synthesizers, or CD writers, or just about anything having "SCSI" in its name other than hard disks, CD-ROMs, or tapes, say yes here. These won't be supported by the kernel directly, so you need some additional software that knows how to talk to these devices using the SCSI protocol.

For scanners, look at SANE *http://www.sane-project.org*. For CD writer software look at Cdrtools, *http://cdrecord.berlios.de/old/ private/cdrecord.html*, and for burning a "disk at once," check out CDRDAO, *http://cdrdao.sourceforge.net*. Cdparanoia is a high-quality digital reader of audio CDs (*http://www.xiph.org/paranoia*). For other devices, it's possible that you'll have to write the driver software yourself. Please read the file *Documentation/scsi/scsi-generic.txt* for more information.

CHR_DEV_SCH SCSI media changer support

This is a driver for SCSI media changers. The most common such devices are tape libraries and MOD/CD-ROM jukeboxes. This option is for real jukeboxes; you don't need it for tiny six-slot CD-ROM changers. Media changers are listed as "Type: Medium Changer" in */proc/scsi/scsi*. Check *Documentation/scsi/scsi-changer. txt* for details.

SCSI_MULTI_ LUN Probe all LUNs on each SCSI device

If you have a SCSI device, such as a CD jukebox, that supports more than one LUN (Logical Unit Number), and only one LUN is detected, you can say yes here to force the SCSI driver to probe for multiple LUNs. A SCSI device with multiple LUNs acts logically like multiple SCSI devices. The vast majority of SCSI devices have only one LUN, and so most people can say no here. The max_luns boot/module parameter allows you to override this setting.

SCSI_SATA   Serial ATA (SATA) support

This driver family supports serial ATA host controllers and devices.

MD   Multiple devices driver support (RAID and LVM)

This option supports multiple physical spindles through a single logical device and is required for RAID and logical volume management.

BLK_DEV_MD   RAID support

This driver lets you combine several hard disk partitions into one logical block device. This can be used to simply append one partition to another one or to combine several redundant hard disks into a RAID 1, RAID 4, or RAID 5 device to provide protection against hard disk failures. This is called *software RAID* because the combining of the partitions is done by the kernel. *Hardware RAID* means that the combining is done by a dedicated controller. If you have such a controller, you do not need to say yes here.

More information about software RAID on Linux is in the "Software RAID" mini-HOWTO, available from *http://www.tldp.org/docs.html#howto*. There you will also learn where to get the supporting userspace *raidtools* utilities.

BLK_DEV_DM   Device mapper support

Device mapper is a low-level volume manager. It works by allowing people to specify mappings for ranges of logical sectors. Various mapping types are available, in addition to which people may write their own modules containing custom mappings.

Higher-level volume managers such as LVM2 use this driver.

IEEE1394   IEEE 1394 (FireWire) support

IEEE 1394 describes a high-performance serial bus, which is also known as FireWire or i.Link and is used for connecting all sorts of devices (most notably, digital video cameras) to your computer.

If you have FireWire hardware and want to use it, say yes here. This is the core support only. You will also need to select a driver for your IEEE 1394 adapter.

I2O   I2O support

The Intelligent Input/Output (I2O) architecture allows hardware drivers to be split into two parts: an operating-system-specific module called the OSM and a hardware-specific module called the HDM. The OSM can talk to a whole range of HDMs, and ideally the HDMs are not OS-dependent. This allows for the same HDM driver to be used under different operating systems if the relevant OSM is in place. In order for this to work, you need to have an I2O interface adapter card in your computer. This card contains a special I/O processor (IOP), allowing high speeds because the CPU does not have to deal with I/O.

If you say yes here, you will get a choice of interface adapter drivers and OSMs and will have to enable the correct ones.

NETDEVICES   Network device support

You can say *no* here if you do not intend to connect your Linux box to any other computer.

You'll have to say yes if your computer contains a network card that you want to use under Linux. If you are going to run SLIP or PPP over a telephone line or null modem cable you also need to say yes here. Connecting two machines with parallel ports using PLIP needs this, as well as AX.25/KISS, for sending Internet traffic over amateur radio links.

See also the *Linux Network Administrator's Guide* by Tony Bautts et al. (O'Reilly), available at *http://www.tldp.org/guides.html*.

NET_ETHERNET   Ethernet (10 or 100 Mbit)

Ethernet (also called IEEE 802.3 or ISO 8802-2) is the most common type of Local Area Network (LAN) in universities and companies.

Common varieties of Ethernet are 10-base2 or Thinnet (10 Mbps over coaxial cable, linking computers in a chain), 10-baseT or twisted pair (10 Mbps over twisted pair cable, linking computers to central hubs), 10-baseF (10 Mbps over optical fiber links, using hubs), 100-baseTX (100 Mbps over two twisted pair cables, using hubs), 100-baseT4 (100 Mbps over four standard voice-grade twisted pair cables, using hubs), 100-baseFX (100 Mbps over optical fiber links), and gigabit Ethernet (1 Gbps over optical fiber or short copper links). The 100-base varieties are also known as Fast Ethernet.

If your Linux machine will be connected to an Ethernet and you have an Ethernet network interface card (NIC) installed in your computer, say yes here and read the Ethernet-HOWTO, available from *http://www.tldp.org/docs.html#howto*. You will then also have to say yes to the driver for your particular NIC.

Note that the answer to this question won't directly affect the kernel: saying *no* will just cause the configurator to skip all the questions about Ethernet network cards.

NET_RADIO

Wireless LAN drivers (non-hamradio) and Wireless Extensions

Support for wireless LANs and everything having to do with packet radio, but not with amateur radio or FM broadcasting.

Saying yes here also enables the Wireless Extensions, creating */proc/net/wireless* and enabling *iwconfig* access. The Wireless Extensions are a generic API that allows a driver to expose configuration and statistics for common wireless LANs to userspace. Wireless Extensions provide a single set of tools that can support all the variations of wireless LANs, regardless of their type (as long as the driver supports Wireless Extensions). Another advantage is that these parameters may be changed on the fly without restarting the driver or operating system. If you wish to use Wireless Extensions with wireless PCMCIA cards (PC cards), you need to say yes here. You can fetch the tools from *http://www.hpl.hp.com/personal/Jean_Tourrilhes/Linux/Tools.html*.

PPP

PPP (Point-to-Point Protocol) support

PPP sends Internet traffic over telephone (and other serial) lines. Ask your access provider if they support it, because otherwise you can't use it. An older protocol with the same purpose is called SLIP. Most Internet access providers these days support PPP rather than SLIP.

To use PPP, you need an additional program called *pppd* as described in the PPP-HOWTO, available at *http://www.tldp.org/docs.html#howto*. Make sure that you have the version of *pppd* recommended in *Documentation/Changes*. The PPP option enlarges your kernel by about 16 KB.

There are actually two versions of PPP: the traditional PPP for asynchronous lines, such as regular analog phone lines, and synchronous PPP, which can be used over digital ISDN lines, for example. If you want to use PPP over phone lines or other asynchronous serial lines, you need to enable the PPP support for async serial ports option.

PPPOE

PPP over Ethernet (experimental)

Support for PPP over Ethernet.

This driver requires the latest version of *pppd* from the CVS repository at *cvs.samba.org*. Alternatively, see the *RoaringPenguin* package *http://www.roaringpenguin.com/pppoe*, which contains instruction on how to use this driver under the heading "Kernel mode PPPoE."

ISDN   ISDN support

ISDN (Integrated Services Digital Networks, called RNIS in France) is a special type of fully digital telephone service; it's mostly used to connect to your Internet service provider (with SLIP or PPP). The main advantage of ISDN is that the speed is higher than ordinary modem/telephone connections and that you can have voice conversations while downloading stuff. It works only if your computer is equipped with an ISDN card and both you and your service provider purchased an ISDN line from the phone company. For details, read *http://www.alumni.caltech.edu/~dank/isdn*.

Select this option if you want your kernel to support ISDN.

PHONE   Linux telephony support

Say yes here if you have a telephony card, which, for example, allows you to use a regular phone for voice over IP applications.

 This option has nothing to do with modems. You do not need to say yes here in order to be able to use a modem under Linux.

INPUT   Generic input layer (needed for keyboard, mouse, ...)

Say yes here if you have any input device (mouse, keyboard, tablet, joystick, steering wheel, etc.) connected to your system and want it to be available to applications. This includes a standard PS/2 keyboard and mouse.

Say no here if you have a headless system (no monitor or keyboard).

More information is available in *Documentation/input/input.txt*.

VT   Virtual terminal

Say yes here to get support for terminal devices with display and keyboard devices. These are called "virtual" because you can run several virtual terminals (also called virtual consoles) on one physical terminal.

You need at least one virtual terminal device in order to make use of your keyboard and monitor. Therefore, only people configuring an embedded system would want to say no here in order to save some memory. The only way to log into such a system is then via a serial or network connection.

Virtual terminals are useful because, for example, one virtual terminal can display system messages and warnings, another one can be used for a text-mode user session, and a third could run an

X session, all in parallel. Switching between virtual terminals is done with certain key combinations, usually Alt-function key.

If you are unsure, say yes, or else you won't be able to do much with your Linux system.

VT_CONSOLE — Support for console on virtual terminal

The system console is the device that receives all kernel messages and warnings and allows logins in single user mode. If you answer yes here, a virtual terminal (the device used to interact with a physical terminal) can be used as system console. This is the most common mode of operations, so you should say yes unless you want the kernel messages be output only to a serial port (in which case you should also enable the console on 8250/16550 and compatible serial port option).

If you say yes here, the currently visible virtual terminal (*/dev/tty0*) will be used as system console by default. You can change that with a kernel command-line option such as `console=tty3`, which specified the third virtual terminal as the system console. (See Chapter 9 for details about how to pass options to the kernel at boot time, and what options are available.)

SERIAL_8250 — 8250/16550 and compatible serial support

This selects whether you want to include the driver for the standard serial ports. The standard answer is yes. People who might say no here are those setting up dedicated Ethernet WWW/FTP servers, or a user that has one of the various bus mice instead of a serial mouse and doesn't intend to use his machine's standard serial port for anything. In addition, the Cyclades and Stallion multiserial port drivers do not need this driver.

 Do not compile this driver as a module if you are using nonstandard serial ports, because the configuration information will be lost when the driver is unloaded. This limitation may be lifted in the future.

Most people will say yes here, so that they can use serial mice, modems, and similar devices connected to the standard serial ports.

AGP — /dev/agpgart (AGP Support)

AGP (Accelerated Graphics Port) is a bus system used mainly to connect graphics cards to the rest of the system.

If you have an AGP system and you say yes here, it will be possible to use the AGP features of your 3D rendering video card. This code acts as a sort of "AGP driver" for the motherboard's chipset.

If you need more texture memory than you can get with the AGP GART (theoretically up to 256 MB, but in practice usually 64 or 128 MB due to kernel allocation issues), you could use PCI accesses and have up to a couple of gigabytes of texture space.

Note that this is the only way to have X and GLX use write-combining with MTRR support on the AGP bus. Without this option, OpenGL direct rendering will be a lot slower, but still faster than PIO.

You should say yes here if you want to use GLX or DRI.

DRM   Direct Rendering Manager (XFree86 4.1.0 and higher DRI support)

Kernel-level support for the Direct Rendering Infrastructure (DRI) was introduced in XFree86 4.0. If you say yes here, you need to select the module that's right for your graphics card from the list. These modules provide support for synchronization, security, and DMA transfers. Please see *http://dri.sourceforge.net* for details. You should also select and configure AGP (*/dev/agpgart*) support.

I2C   I2C support

I2C (pronounced "I-square-C") is a slow serial bus protocol developed by Philips and used in many micro controller applications. SMBus, or System Management Bus, is a subset of the I2C protocol. More information is contained in the directory *Documentation/i2c*, especially in the file there called *summary*.

Both I2C and SMBus are supported by this option. You will need it for hardware sensors support and Video For Linux support.

If you want I2C support, in addition to saying yes here, you must also select the specific drivers for your bus adapters.

SPI   SPI support

The Serial Peripheral Interface (SPI) is a low-level synchronous protocol. Chips that support SPI can have data transfer rates up to several tens of Mbps. Chips are addressed with a controller and a chipselect. Most SPI slaves don't support dynamic device discovery; some are even write-only or read-only.

SPI is widely used by microcontrollers to talk with sensors, EEPROM and flash memory, codecs and various other controller chips, analog-to-digital and digital-to-analog converters, and more. MMC and SD cards can be accessed using SPI protocol, and for DataFlash cards used in MMC sockets, SPI must always be used.

SPI is one of a family of similar protocols using a four-wire interface (select, clock, data in, and data out), including Microwire (half duplex), SSP, SSI, and PSP. This driver framework should work with most such devices and controllers.

HWMON Hardware-monitoring support

Hardware-monitoring devices let you monitor the hardware health of a system. Most modern motherboards include such a device. It may include temperature sensors, voltage sensors, fan speed sensors, and various additional features such as the ability to control the speed of the fans. If you want this support you should say yes here and also to the specific driver for your sensor chip.

VIDEO_DEV Video for Linux

This option enables support for audio/video capture and overlay devices and FM radio cards. The exact capabilities of each device vary.

The kernel includes support for the new Video for Linux Two API, (V4L2) as well as the original system. Drivers and applications need to be rewritten to use V4L2, but drivers for popular cards and applications for most video capture functions already exist.

Additional info and docs are available at *http://linuxtv.org*. Documentation for V4L2 is also available at *http://bytesex.org/v4l*.

DVB DVB for Linux

This option enables support for Digital Video Broadcasting hardware. Enable this if you own a DVB adapter and want to use it or if you are compiling Linux for a digital set-top box.

API specs and user tools are available from *http://www.linuxtv.org*.

FB Support for frame buffer devices

The frame buffer device provides an abstraction for the graphics hardware. It represents the frame buffer of some video hardware and allows application software to access the graphics hardware through a well-defined interface, so the software doesn't need to know anything about the low-level (hardware register) stuff.

Frame buffer devices work identically across the different architectures supported by Linux and make the implementation of application programs easier and more portable. At this point, an X server exists that uses the frame buffer device exclusively. On several non-X86 architectures, the frame buffer device is the only way to use the graphics hardware.

You need a program called *fbset* to make full use of frame buffer devices. Please read *Documentation/fb/framebuffer.txt* and the Framebuffer-HOWTO, available at *http://www.tldp.org/HOWTO/ Framebuffer-HOWTO.html* for more information.

Say yes here and to the driver for your graphics board if you are compiling a kernel for a non-x86 architecture. If you are compiling for the x86 architecture, you can say yes if you want to use the frame buffer, but it is not essential.

Please note that running graphical applications that directly touch the hardware (e.g., an accelerated X server) and that are not attuned to the frame buffer device may cause unexpected results.

VGA_CONSOLE   VGA text console

Saying yes here will allow you to use Linux in text mode through a display that complies with the generic VGA standard. Virtually everyone wants that.

The program SVGATextMode can be used to utilize SVGA video cards to their full potential in text mode. Download it from *ftp:// ibiblio.org/pub/Linux/utils/console*.

LOGO   Bootup logo

This option enables the pretty penguin logo at boot time. It will show up on the frame buffer while the kernel is booting. The number of penguins shows the number of processors that the kernel has found.

SOUND   Sound card support

If you have a sound card in your computer—i.e., if it can create more than an isolated beep—say yes. Be sure to have all the information about your sound card and its configuration (I/O port, interrupt and DMA channel), because you will be asked for it.

Read the Sound-HOWTO, available from *http://www.tldp.org/docs. html#howto*. General information about the modular sound system is contained in the file *Documentation/sound/oss/Introduction*. The file *Documentation/sound/oss/README.OSS* contains some slightly outdated but still useful information as well. Newer sound driver documentation can be found in files in the *Documentation/sound/ alsa* directory.

If you have a PnP sound card and you want to configure it at boot time using the ISA PnP tools (read *http://www.roestock.demon.co. uk/isapnptools*), you need to compile sound card support as a module and load that module after the PnP configuration is finished. To do this properly, read *Documentation/sound/oss/ README.modules*.

I'm told that even without a sound card, you can make your computer create more than an occasional beep by programming the PC speaker. Kernel patches and supporting utilities to do that are in the *pcsp* package, available at *ftp://ftp.infradead.org/pub/pcsp*.

SND　　　　　Advanced Linux Sound Architecture

Say yes to enable ALSA (Advanced Linux Sound Architecture), the standard Linux sound system.

For more information, see *http://www.alsa-project.org*.

SND_USB_　　USB Audio/MIDI driver
AUDIO
Say yes here to include support for USB audio and USB MIDI devices.

USB　　　　　Support for host-side USB

Universal Serial Bus (USB) is a specification for a serial bus subsystem that offers higher speeds and more features than the traditional PC serial port. The bus supplies power to peripherals and allows for hot swapping. Up to 127 USB peripherals can be connected to a single USB host in a tree structure.

The USB host is the root of the tree, the peripherals are the leaves, and the inner nodes are special USB devices called hubs. Most PCs now have USB host ports, used to connect peripherals such as scanners, keyboards, mice, modems, cameras, disks, flash memory, network links, and printers to the PC.

Say yes here if your computer has a host-side USB port and you want to use USB devices. You then need to say yes to at least one of the Host Controller Driver (HCD) options that follow. Choose a USB 1.1 controller, such as UHCI HCD support or OHCI HCD support, and EHCI HCD (USB 2.0) support except for older systems that do not have USB 2.0 support. It does not hurt to select them all if you are not certain.

If your system has a device-side USB port, used in the peripheral side of the USB protocol, see the USB Gadget option instead.

After choosing your HCD, select drivers for the USB peripherals you'll be using. You may want to check out the information provided in *Documentation/usb* and especially the links given in *Documentation/usb/usb-help.txt*.

USB_EHCI_HCD　　EHCI HCD (USB 2.0) support

The Enhanced Host Controller Interface (EHCI) is standard for USB 2.0 "high-speed" (480 Mbit/sec, 60 Mbyte/sec) host controller hardware. If your USB host controller supports USB 2.0, you will likely want to configure this HCD. At the time of this writing, the primary implementation of EHCI is a chip from NEC, widely available in add-on PCI cards, but implementations are in the works from other vendors, including Intel and Philips. Motherboard support is emerging.

EHCI controllers are packaged with "companion" host controllers (OHCI or UHCI) to handle USB 1.1 devices connected to root hub ports. Ports will connect to EHCI if the device is high-speed; otherwise, they connect to a companion controller. If you configure EHCI, you should probably configure the OHCI (for NEC and some other vendors) USB HCD or UHCI (for VIA motherboards) HCD, too.

You may want to read *Documentation/usb/ehci.txt* for more information on this driver.

USB_OHCI_HCD   OHCI HCD support

The Open Host Controller Interface (OHCI) is a standard for accessing USB 1.1 host controller hardware. It does more in hardware than Intel's UHCI specification. If your USB host controller follows the OHCI spec, say yes. On most non-x86 systems, and on x86 hardware that's not using a USB controller from Intel or VIA, this is appropriate. If your host controller doesn't use PCI, this is probably appropriate. For a PCI-based system where you're not sure, the *lspci -v* command will list the right prog-if for your USB controller(s): EHCI, OHCI, or UHCI.

USB_UHCI_HCD   UHCI HCD (most Intel and VIA) support

The Universal Host Controller Interface is a standard created by Intel for accessing the USB hardware in the PC (which is also called the USB host controller). If your USB host controller conforms to this standard, you may want to say yes. All recent boards with Intel PCI chipsets (such as Intel 430TX, 440FX, 440LX, 440BX, i810, i820) conform to this standard. All VIA PCI chipsets (like VIA VP2, VP3, MVP3, Apollo Pro, Apollo Pro II, or Apollo Pro 133) also use the standard.

USB_STORAGE   USB mass storage support

Say yes here if you want to connect USB mass storage devices to your computer's USB port. This is the driver you need for USB floppy drives, USB hard disks, USB tape drives, USB CD-ROMs, USB flash devices, and memory sticks, along with similar devices. This driver may also be used for some cameras and card readers.

This option enables the SCSI option, but you probably also need SCSI device support: SCSI disk support for most USB storage devices to work properly.

USB_SERIAL   USB serial converter support

Say yes here if you have a USB device that provides normal serial ports, or acts like a serial device, and you want to connect it to your USB bus.

Please read *Documentation/usb/usb-serial.txt* for more information on the specifics of the different devices that are supported and on how to use them.

USB_GADGET   Support for USB gadgets

USB is a master/slave protocol, organized with one master host (such as a PC) controlling up to 127 peripheral devices. The USB hardware is asymmetric, which makes it easier to set up: you can't connect a "to-the-host" connector to a peripheral.

Linux can run in the host or in the peripheral. In both cases you need a low-level bus controller driver and some software that talks to it. Peripheral controllers can be either discrete silicon or integrated with the CPU in a microcontroller. The more familiar host-side controllers have names like such as EHCI, OHCI, or UHCI, and are usually integrated into southbridges on PC motherboards.

Enable this configuration option if you want to run Linux inside a USB peripheral device. Configure one hardware driver for your peripheral/device side bus controller, and a "gadget driver" for your peripheral protocol. (If you use modular gadget drivers, you may configure more than one.)

If in doubt, say no and don't enable these drivers; most people don't have this kind of hardware (except maybe inside Linux PDAs).

For more information, see *http://www.linux-usb.org/gadget* and the kernel DocBook documentation for this API.

MMC   MMC support

MMC is the MultiMediaCard bus protocol.

If you want MMC support, you should say yes here and also to the specific driver for your MMC interface.

INFINIBAND   InfiniBand support

Core support for InfiniBand. Make sure to also select any protocols you wish to use as well as drivers for your InfiniBand hardware.

EDAC   EDAC core system error reporting (experimental)

EDAC is designed to report errors in the core system. These are low-level errors that are reported by the CPU or supporting chipset: memory errors, cache errors, PCI errors, thermal throttling, etc.

If this code is reporting problems on your system, please see the EDAC project web pages for more information: *http://bluesmoke. sourceforge.net* and *http://buttersideup.com/edacwiki*.

EXT2_FS   Second extended filesystem support

ext2 is a standard Linux filesystem for hard disks. Most systems use the upgrade, *ext3*, instead.

 Note that the filesystem of your root partition (the one containing the directory /) cannot be compiled as a module without using a special boot process, so building it as a module could be dangerous.

EXT3_FS   Third extended filesystem support

This is the journaling version (called *ext3*) of the second extended filesystem, the de facto standard Linux filesystem for hard disks.

The journaling code included in this driver means you do not have to run *fsck* (filesystem checker) on your filesystems after a crash. The journal keeps track of any changes that were being made at the time the system crashed, and can ensure that your filesystem is consistent without the need for a lengthy check.

Other than adding the journal to the filesystem, the on-disk format of *ext3* is identical to *ext2*. It is possible to freely switch between using the *ext3* driver and the *ext2* driver, as long as the filesystem has been cleanly unmounted, or *fsck* is run on the filesystem before the switch.

To add a journal on an existing *ext2* filesystem or change the behavior of *ext3* filesystems, you can use the *tune2fs* utility. To modify attributes of files and directories on *ext3* filesystems, use *chattr*. You need *e2fsprogs* version 1.20 or later in order to create *ext3* journals (available at *http://sourceforge.net/projects/e2fsprogs*).

REISERFS_FS   ReiserFS support

This is a journaled filesystem that stores not just filenames but the files themselves in a balanced tree. Balanced trees can be more efficient than traditional filesystem architectural foundations.

In general, ReiserFS is as fast as *ext2*, but is more efficient with large directories and small files.

JFS_FS   JFS filesystem support

This is a port of IBM's Journaled Filesystem (JFS). More information is available in the file *Documentation/filesystems/jfs.txt*.

XFS_FS   XFS filesystem support

XFS is a high-performance journaling filesystem that originated on the SGI IRIX platform. It is completely multithreaded; supports large files and large filesystems, extended attributes, and variable block sizes; is extent-based; makes extensive use of B-trees; and uses directories, extents, and free space to aid both performance and scalability.

Refer to the documentation at *http://oss.sgi.com/projects/xfs* for complete details. This implementation is on-disk compatible with the IRIX version of XFS.

OCFS2_FS   OCFS2 filesystem support (experimental)

OCFS2 is a general-purpose, extent-based, shared-disk cluster file-system with many similarities to *ext3*. It supports 64-bit inode numbers and has automatically extending metadata groups, which may also make it attractive for nonclustered use.

You'll want to install the *ocfs2-tools* package in order to at least get the *mount.ocfs2* program.

The project web page is *http://oss.oracle.com/projects/ocfs2* and the tools web page is *http://oss.oracle.com/projects/ocfs2-tools*. OCFS2 mailing lists can be found at *http://oss.oracle.com/projects/ocfs2/mailman*.

INOTIFY   inotify file change notification support

Say yes here to enable inotify support and the associated system calls. inotify is a file change notification system and a replacement for dnotify. inotify fixes numerous shortcomings in dnotify and introduces several new features. It allows monitoring of both files and directories via a single open fd object. Other features include multiple file events, one-shot support, and unmount notification.

For more information, see *Documentation/filesystems/inotify.txt*.

QUOTA   Quota support

If you say yes here, you will be able to set per-user limits for disk usage (also called disk quotas). Currently, it works for the *ext2*, *ext3*, and ReiserFS filesystem. *ext3* also supports journaled quotas, for which you don't need to run *quotacheck* after an unclean shutdown. For further details, read the "Quota" mini-HOWTO, available from *http://www.tldp.org/docs.html#howto* or the documentation provided with the quota tools. Quota support is probably useful only for multiuser systems.

AUTOFS_FS   Kernel automounter support

The automounter is a tool that automatically mounts remote file-systems on demand. This implementation is partially kernel-based to reduce overhead when a system is already mounted. This is unlike the BSD automounter (*amd*), which is a pure userspace daemon.

To use the automounter, you need the userspace tools from the autofs package; you can find the location in *Documentation/ Changes*. You also want to answer yes to the NFS filesystem support option.

If you want to use the newer version of the automounter with more features, say no here and say yes to the Kernel automounter v4 support option.

If you are not a part of a fairly large, distributed network, you probably do not need an automounter, and can say no here.

FUSE_FS Filesystem in userspace support

With FUSE it is possible to implement a fully functional filesystem in a userspace program.

There's also companion library named *libfuse*. This library, along with utilities, is available from the FUSE homepage: *http://fuse. sourceforge.net*.

See *Documentation/filesystems/fuse.txt* for more information. See *Documentation/Changes for library/utility* version you need.

If you want to develop a userspace filesystem, or if you want to use a filesystem based on FUSE, answer yes here.

SMB_FS SMB filesystem support (to mount Windows shares etc.)

SMB (Server Message Block) is the protocol Windows for Workgroups (WfW), Windows 95/98, Windows NT and later variants, and OS/2 LAN Manager use to share files and printers over local networks. Saying yes here allows you to mount their filesystems (often called "shares" in this context) and access them just like any other Unix directory. Currently, this works only if the Windows machines use TCP/IP as the underlying transport protocol, not NetBEUI. For details, read *Documentation/filesystems/smbfs.txt* and the SMB-HOWTO, available from *http://www.tldp.org/docs. html#howto*.

If you just want your box to act as an SMB server and make files and printing services available to Windows clients (which need to have a TCP/IP stack), you don't need to say yes here; you can use the Samba set of daemons and programs (available from *ftp://ftp. samba.org/pub/samba*).

CIFS CIFS support (advanced network filesystem for Samba, Window, and other CIFS compliant servers)

This is the client VFS module for the Common Internet File System (CIFS) protocol, which is the successor to the Server Message Block (SMB) protocol, the native file-sharing mechanism for most early PC operating systems. The CIFS protocol is fully supported by file servers such as Windows 2000 (including Windows 2003, NT 4, and Windows XP) as well by Samba (which provides excellent CIFS server support for Linux and many other operating systems). Limited support for Windows ME and similar servers is provided as well. You must use the *smbfs* client filesystem to access older SMB servers such as OS/2 and DOS.

The intent of the *cifs* module is to provide an advanced network filesystem client for mounting local filesystems to CIFS-compliant servers, including support for DFS (hierarchical namespace), secure per-user session establishment, safe distributed caching (*oplock*), optional packet signing, Unicode and other internationalization improvements, and optional Winbind (*nsswitch*) integration. You do not need to enable *cifs* if you are running only a server (Samba). It is possible to enable both *smbfs* and *cifs* (e.g., if you are using CIFS for accessing Windows 2003 and Samba 3 servers, and *smbfs* for accessing old servers). If you need to mount to Samba or Windows from this machine, say yes to this option.

PROFILING   Profiling support (experimental)

Say yes here to enable the extended profiling support mechanisms used by profilers such as OProfile.

OPROFILE   OProfilesystem profiling (experimental)

OProfile is a profiling system capable of profiling the whole system, including the kernel, kernel modules, libraries, and applications.

For more information and links to the userspace tools needed to use OProfile properly, see the main project page at *http://oprofile. sourceforge.net/news*.

KPROBES   Kprobes (experimental)

Kprobes allows you to trap the CPU at almost any kernel address and execute a callback function. register_kprobe( ) establishes a probepoint and specifies the callback. Kprobes is useful for kernel debugging, nonintrusive instrumentation, and testing.

PRINTK_TIME   Show timing information on printks

Selecting this option causes timing information to be included in printk (kernel message) output. This allows you to measure the interval between kernel operations, including bootup operations. This is useful for identifying long delays in kernel startup.

MAGIC_SYSRQ   Magic SysRq key

If you say yes here, you will have some control over the system even if the system crashes for example during kernel debugging (i.e., you will be able to flush the buffer cache to disk, reboot the system immediately, or dump some status information). This is accomplished by pressing various keys while holding down the SysRq (Alt+PrintScreen) key. It also works on a serial console (on PC hardware at least), if you send a BREAK and then within 5 seconds a command keypress. The keys are documented in *Documentation/sysrq.txt*. Don't say yes unless you really know what this hack does.

DEBUG_KERNEL   Kernel debugging

Say yes here if you are developing drivers or trying to debug and identify kernel problems.

On its own, this option does not do anything except allow you to chance to select other options.

DEBUG_FS   Debug filesystem

debugfs is a virtual filesystem where kernel developers put debugging files. Enable this option to be able to read and write to these files.

SECURITY   Enable different security models

This allows you to configure different security modules into your kernel.

If this option is not selected, the default Linux security model will be used.

SECURITY_
SELINUX   NSA SELinux support

This selects NSA Security-Enhanced Linux (SELinux). You will also need a policy configuration and a labeled filesystem. You can obtain the policy compiler (*checkpolicy*), the utility for labeling filesystems (*setfiles*), and an example policy configuration from *http://www.nsa.gov/selinux*.

IV

Additional Information

This section includes an Appendix about useful utilities, and pointers to further information.

A

Helpful Utilities

Retrieving, building, updating, and maintaining a Linux kernel source tree involves a lot of different steps, as this book shows. Being naturally lazy creatures, developers have created some programs to help with the various routine tasks. Here we describe a few of these useful tools and the basics on how to use them.

Linux kernel development differs in many ways from traditional software development. Some of the special demands on kernel programmers include:

- Constantly applying your changes to the moving target of a fast-based kernel development release schedule
- Resolving any merge conflicts between changes you have made and changes made by other people
- Exporting your changes in a format that lets others incorporate and work with it easily

patch and diff

This section is based on an article originally published in *Linux Journal*.

One of the most common methods of doing kernel work is to use the *patch* and *diff* programs. To use these tools, two different directory trees: a "clean" one and a "working" one must be used. The clean tree is a released kernel version, while the working one is based on the same version but contains your modifications. Then you can use *patch* and *diff* to extract your changes and port them forward to a new kernel release.

For an example, create two directories containing the latest kernel version as described in Chapter 3:

```
$ tar -zxf linux-2.6.19.tar.gz
$ mv linux-2.6.19 linux-2.6.19-dirty
```

```
$ tar -zxf linux-2.6.19.tar.gz
$ ls
linux-2.6.19/
linux-2.6.19-dirty/
```

Now make all of the different changes you wish to do in the -*dirty* directory and leave the clean, original kernel directory alone. After finishing making changes, you should create a patch to send it to other people:

```
$ diff -Naur -X linux-2.6.19/Documentation/dontdiff linux-2.6.19/ \
linux-2.6.19-dirty/ > my_patch
```

This will create a file called *my_patch* that contains the difference between your work and a clean 2.6.19 kernel tree. This patch then can be sent to other people via email.

New Kernel Versions

If a new kernel version is released, and you wish to port your changes to the new version, you need to try to apply your generated patch onto a clean kernel version. This can be done in the following steps:

1. Generate your original patch, as in the previous example.

2. Using the official patch from *kernel.org*, move the old kernel version forward one release:

```
$ cd linux-2.6.19
$ patch -p1 < ../patch-2.6.20
$ cd ..
$ mv linux-2.6.19 linux-2.6.20
```

3. Move your working directory forward one release by removing your patch, then apply the new update:

```
$ cd linux-2.6.19-dirty
$ patch -p1 -R < ../my_patch
$ patch -p1 < ../patch-2.6.20
$ cd ..
$ mv linux-2.4.19-dirty linux-2.6.20-dirty
```

4. Try to apply your patch on top of the new update:

```
$ cd linux-2.6.20-dirty
$ patch -p1 < ../my_patch
```

If your patch does not apply cleanly, resolve all of the conflicts that are created (the *patch* command will tell you about these conflicts, leaving behind *.rej* and *.orig* files for you to compare and fix up manually using your favorite editor). This merge process can be the most difficult part if you have made changes to portions of the source tree that have been changed by other people.

If you use this development process, I highly recommend getting the excellent *patchutils* set of programs (found at *http://cyberelk.net/tim/patchutils*). These programs enable you to manipulate text patches easily in all sorts of useful ways, and have saved kernel developers many hours of tedious work.

Managing Your Patches with quilt

Kernel development using *patch* and *diff* generally works quite well. But after a while, most people grow tired of it and look for a different way to work that does not involve so much tedious patching and merging. Luckily, a few kernel developers came up with a program called *quilt* that handles the process of manipulating a number of patches made against an external source tree much easier.

The idea for *quilt* came from a set of scripts written by Andrew Morton that he used to first maintain the memory management subsystem and then later the entire development kernel tree. His scripts were tied very tightly to his workflow, but the ideas behind them were very powerful. Andreas Gruenbacher took those ideas and created the *quilt* tool.

The basic idea behind *quilt* is that you work with a pristine source tree and add a bunch of patches on top of it. You can push and pop different patches off of the source tree, and maintain this list of patches in a simple manner.

1. To get started, create a kernel source tree like always:

   ```
   $ tar -zxf linux-2.6.19.tar.gz
   $ ls
   linux-2.6.19/
   ```

2. And go into that directory:

   ```
   $ cd linux-2.6.19
   ```

3. To get started, create a directory called *patches* that will hold all of our kernel patches:

   ```
   $ mkdir patches
   ```

4. Then tell *quilt* to create a new patch called *patch1*:

   ```
   $ quilt new patch1
   Patch patches/patch1 is now on top
   ```

5. *quilt* needs to be told about all of the different files that will be modifed by this new patch. To do this, use the *add* command:

   ```
   $ quilt add Makefile
   File Makefile added to patch patches/patch1
   ```

6. Edit the file *Makefile*, modify the EXTRAVERSION line, and save the change. After you finish, tell *quilt* to refresh the patch:

   ```
   $ quilt refresh
   Refreshed patch patches/patch1
   ```

The file *patches/patch1* will contain a patch with the changes that you have just made:

```
$ cat patches/patch1
Index: linux-2.6.19/Makefile
===================================================================
--- linux-2.6.19.orig/Makefile
+++ linux-2.6.19/Makefile
@@ -1,7 +1,7 @@
 VERSION = 2
```

```
 PATCHLEVEL = 6
 SUBLEVEL = 19
-EXTRAVERSION =
+EXTRAVERSION = -dirty
 NAME=Crazed Snow-Weasel

 # *DOCUMENTATION*
```

You can continue on, working with this single patch, or create a new one to go on top of this patch. As an example, if three different patches had been created, patch1, patch2, and patch3, they will be applied one on top of one another.

To see the list of patches that are currently applied:

```
$ quilt series -v
+ patches/patch1
+ patches/patch2
= patches/patch3
```

This output shows that all three patches are applied, and that the current one is patch3.

If a new kernel version is released, and you wish to port your changes to the new version, quilt can handle this easily with the following steps:

1. Pop off all of the patches that are currently on the tree:

```
$ quilt pop -a
Removing patch patches/patch3
Restoring drivers/usb/Makefile
Removing patch patches/patch2
Restoring drivers/Makefile
Removing patch patches/patch1
Restoring Makefile
No patches applied
```

2. Using the official patch from *kernel.org*, move the old kernel version forward one release:

```
$ patch -p1 < ../patch-2.6.20
$ cd ..
$ mv linux-2.6.19 linux-2.6.20
```

3. Now have quilt push all of the patches back on top of the new tree:

```
$ quilt push
Applying patch patches/patch1
patching file Makefile
Hunk #1 FAILED at 1.
1 out of 1 hunk FAILED -- rejects in file Makefile
Patch patches/patch1 does not apply (enforce with -f)
```

4. As the first patch doesn't apply cleanly, force the patch to be applied and then fix it up:

```
$ quilt push -f
Applying patch patches/patch1
patching file Makefile
Hunk #1 FAILED at 1.
1 out of 1 hunk FAILED -- saving rejects to file Makefile.rej
```

```
Applied patch patches/patch1 (forced; needs refresh)
$ vim Makefile.rej Makefile
```

5. After the patch is applied by hand, refresh the patch:

```
$ quilt refresh
Refreshed patch patches/patch1
```

6. And continue pushing the other patches:

```
$ quilt push
Applying patch patches/patch2
patching file drivers/Makefile
Now at patch patches/patch2
$ quilt push
Applying patch patches/patch3
patching file drivers/usb/Makefile
Now at patch patches/patch3
```

quilt also has options that will automatically email out all of the patches in the series to a group of people or a mailing list, delete specific patches in the middle of the series, go up or down the series of patches until a specific patch is found, and many more powerful options.

If you want to do any kind of kernel development, *quilt* is strongly recommended, even for tracking a few patches, instead of using the more difficult *diff* and *patch* method. It is much simpler and will save you much time and effort.

On a personal note, I cannot recommend this tool enough, as I use it everyday to manage hundreds of patches in different development trees. It is also used by numerous Linux distributions to maintain their kernel packages and has an involved and responsive development community.

git

git is a source code control tool that was originally written by Linus Torvalds when the Linux kernel was looking for a new source code control system. It is a distributed system, which differs from traditional source code control systems such as CVS in that it is not required to be connected to a server in order to make a commit to the repository.

git is one of the most powerful, flexible, and fast source code control systems currently available, and has an active development team working behind it. The main web page for *git* can be found at *http://git.or.cz/*. It is recommended that any new user of *git* go through the published tutorials in order to become familiar with how *git* works, and how to use it properly.

The Linux kernel is developed using *git*, and the latest *git* kernel tree can be found at *http://www.kernel.org/git/*, along with a large list of other kernel developer's *git* repositories.

It is not necessary to use *git* in order to do Linux kernel development, but it is very handy in helping to track down kernel bugs. If you report a bug to the Linux kernel developers, they might ask you to use *git bisect* in order to find the exact change that caused the bug to happen. If so, follow the directions in the *git* documentation for how to use this.

ketchup

ketchup is a very handy tool used to update or switch between different versions of the Linux kernel source tree. It has the ability to:

- Find the latest version of the kernel, download it, and uncompress it.
- Update a currently installed version of the kernel source tree to any other version, by patching the tree to the proper version.
- Handle the different development and stable branches of the kernel tree, including the *-mm* and *-stable* trees.
- Download any patches or tarballs needed to do the update, if they are not present on the machine already.
- Check the GPG signatures of the tarball and patches to verify that it has downloaded a correct file.

ketchup can be found at *http://www.selenic.com/ketchup/* and has lots of additional documentation in the wiki at *http://www.selenic.com/ketchup/wiki/*.

Here is a set of steps that show how simple it is to use *ketchup* to download a specific kernel version, and then have it switch the directory to another kernel version with only a minimal number of commands.

To have *ketchup* download the 2.6.16.24 version of the kernel source tree into a directory, and rename the directory to be the same as the kernel version, enter:

```
$ mkdir foo
$ cd foo
$ ketchup -r 2.6.16.24
None -> 2.6.16.24
Unpacking linux-2.6.17.tar.bz2
Applying patch-2.6.17.bz2 -R
Applying patch-2.6.16.24.bz2
Current directory renamed to /home/gregkh/linux/linux-2.6.16.24
```

Now, to upgrade this kernel to contain the latest stable kernel version, just enter:

```
$ ketchup -r 2.6
2.6.16.24 -> 2.6.17.11
Applying patch-2.6.16.24.bz2 -R
Applying patch-2.6.17.bz2
Downloading patch-2.6.17.11.bz2
--22:21:14--  http://www.kernel.org/pub/linux/kernel/v2.6/patch-2.6.17.11.
bz2
             => `/home/greg/.ketchup/patch-2.6.17.11.bz2.partial'
Resolving www.kernel.org... 204.152.191.37, 204.152.191.5
Connecting to www.kernel.org|204.152.191.37|:80... connected.
HTTP request sent, awaiting response... 200 OK
Length: 36,809 (36K) [application/x-bzip2]
100%[====================================>] 36,809         93.32K/s
22:21:14 (92.87 KB/s) - `/home/greg/.ketchup/patch-2.6.17.11.bz2.partial'
saved [36809/36809]
Downloading patch-2.6.17.11.bz2.sign
```

```
--22:21:14-- http://www.kernel.org/pub/linux/kernel/v2.6/patch-2.6.17.11.
bz2.sign
              => `/home/greg/.ketchup/patch-2.6.17.11.bz2.sign.partial'
Resolving www.kernel.org... 204.152.191.37, 204.152.191.5
Connecting to www.kernel.org|204.152.191.37|:80... connected.
HTTP request sent, awaiting response... 200 OK
Length: 248 [application/pgp-signature]
100%[=====================================>] 248           --.--K/s
22:21:14 (21.50 MB/s) - `/home/greg/.ketchup/patch-2.6.17.11.bz2.sign.
partial' saved [248/248]
Verifying signature...
gpg: Signature made Wed Aug 23 15:01:04 2006 PDT using DSA key ID 517D0F0E
gpg: Good signature from "Linux Kernel Archives Verification Key >
ftpadmin@kernel.org<"
gpg: WARNING: This key is not certified with a trusted signature!
gpg:          There is no indication that the signature belongs to the
owner.
Primary key fingerprint: C75D C40A 11D7 AF88 9981  ED5B C86B A06A 517D 0F0E
Applying patch-2.6.17.11.bz2
Current directory renamed to /home/greg/linux/tmp/x/linux-2.6.17.11
```

This shows that *ketchup* automatically determined that the newest stable version was 2.6.17.11 and downloaded the needed patch files in order to get to that version.

It is highly recommended that you use *ketchup* if you want to download any Linux kernel source trees. It takes all of the work in finding where on the server the correct patch file is, and automatically applies the patch in the proper format, after checking that the downloaded file is properly signed. Combine *ketchup* with *quilt* and you have a very powerful setup that contains everything that you need in order to deal effectively with kernel sources as a Linux kernel developer.

B

Bibliography

Most of the information in this book has been extracted from the kernel documentation and source code. This is the best place for information on how to build and install the kernel and is usually kept up to date when things in the build procedure change.

Books

There are a number of very good Linux kernel programming books available, but only a few that deal with building and installing the kernel. Here is a list of books that I have found useful when dealing with the Linux kernel.

General Linux Books

Ellen Siever, Aaron Weber, Stephen Figgins, Robert Love, and Arnold Robbins. *Linux in a Nutshell* (O'Reilly), 2005.

> This book has the most complete and authoritative command reference for Linux. It covers almost every single command that you will ever need to use.

Yaghmour, Karim. *Building Embedded Linux Systems* (O'Reilly), 2003.

> This book, although mainly oriented toward the embedded Linux developer, has a great section on how to build up a cross-compiler toolchain and kernel. It is highly recommended for that section, as well as for other portions of the book that are valuable to people wishing to learn more about how to customize a Linux kernel and the rest of the system.

Linux Kernel Books

Most of these books are oriented toward the programmer who is interested in learning how to program within the kernel. They are much more technically oriented than this book, but are a great place to start if you wish to learn more about the code that controls the kernel.

Jonathan Corbet, Alessandro Rubini, and Greg Kroah-Hartman. *Linux Device Drivers* (O'Reilly), 2005.

> This book covers how the different kernel device driver subsystems work, and provides lots of examples of working drivers. It is recommended for anyone wanting to work with Linux kernel drivers. It is also available online for free at *http://lwn.net/Kernel/LDD3/*.

Love, Robert. *Linux Kernel Development* (Novell Press Publishing), 2005.

> Robert Love's book covers almost all areas of the Linux kernel, showing how everything works together. It is a great place to start learning about the different portions of the kernel internals.

Bovet, Daniel P. and Cesate, Marco. *Understanding the Linux Kernel* (O'Reilly), 2005.

> This book goes into the design and implementation of the core Linux kernel. It is a great reference for understanding the algorithms used within the different portions of the kernel. It is highly recommended for anyone wanting to understand the details of how the kernel works.

Bibliography

Tool Locations

A lot of different tools were mentioned in this book. Here are links to where the source code for these tools can be found on the Internet.

Linux kernel
> *http://www.kernel.org* and *ftp://ftp.kernel.org* contain all of the different versions of the Linux kernel source code. *http://www.kernel.org/git/* contains a listing of all *git* trees in use by the different kernel developers.

gcc
> *http://gcc.gnu.org/* is the main site for everything related to the GNU C Compiler.

binutils
> *http://www.gnu.org/software/binutils/* is the main site for all information about *binutils*.

make
> *http://www.gnu.org/software/make/* is the main site for all information about *make*.

util-linux
> *http://www.kernel.org/pub/linux/utils/util-linux/* is the directory where all versions of *util-linux* can be downloaded.

module-init-tools

> http://www.kernel.org/pub/linux/utils/kernel/module-init-tools/ is the directory where all versions of *module-init-tools* can be downloaded.

e2fsprogs

> http://e2fsprogs.sourceforge.net/ is the main project page for the *e2fsprogs* package.

jfsutils

> http://jfs.sourceforge.net/ is the main project page for the *jfsutils* package.

reiserfsprogs

> http://www.namesys.com/download.html is the main project page for the *reiserfsprogs* package.

xfsprogs

> http://oss.sgi.com/projects/xfs/ is the main project page for the *xfsprogs* package.

quota-tools

> http://sourceforge.net/projects/linuxquota/ is the main project page for the *quota-tools* package.

nfs-utils

> http://nfs.sf.net/ is the main project page for the *nfs-utils* package.

udev

> http://www.kernel.org/pub/linux/utils/kernel/hotplug/udev.html is the directory where all versions of *udev* can be downloaded.

procfs

> http://procps.sourceforge.net/ is the main project page for the *procfs* package.

patchutils

> http://cyberelk.net/tim/patchutils is the location for all of the *patchutils* releases.

git

> http://git.or.cz/ is the main site for the *git* project.

ketchup

> http://www.selenic.com/ketchup/ is the main project page for the *ketchup* program.

quilt

> http://savannah.nongnu.org/projects/quilt is the main project page for the *quilt* program.

distcc

> http://distcc.samba.org/ is the main project page for the *distcc* program.

ccache

> http://ccache.samba.org/ is the main project page for the *ccache* program.

Index

We'd like to hear your suggestions for improving our indexes. Send email to *index@oreilly.com*.

About the Author

Greg Kroah-Hartman has been building the Linux kernel since 1996 and started writing Linux kernel drivers in 1999. He is currently the maintainer of the USB, PCI, driver core, and *sysfs* subsystems in the kernel source tree and is also one half of the *-stable* kernel release team. He created the *udev* program and maintains the Linux hotplug userspace project. He is a Gentoo Linux developer as well as the coauthor of the third edition of *Linux Device Drivers* (O'Reilly) and a contributing editor to *Linux Journal*. He also created and maintains the Linux Device Driver Kit. He currently works for SUSE Labs/Novell, doing various Linux kernel-related tasks.

Colophon

The animal on the cover of *Linux Kernel in a Nutshell* is a cup coral (*Balanophyllia elegans*). Most commonly found on or under shaded rocks, cup corals range from British Columbia to Baja, California. Cup corals are generally orange in color, with lighter orange tentacles extending out from the stony skeleton base.

Cup corals are armed with tentacles that have clusters of poisoning stingers called spirocysts, which they use to prey on passing plankton. Once plankton is captured, the coral will use its tentacles to draw the food into its stomach. Cup corals also use their tentacles to attach themselves to rocks.

The cover image is from *Riverside Natural History*. The cover font is Adobe ITC Garamond. The text font is Linotype Birka; the heading font is Adobe Myriad Condensed; and the code font is LucasFont's TheSans Mono Condensed.

How much memory used by kernel =
total amount of memory minus
`total mem` in /proc/meminfo or
the output of `free`

To redirect output of 'make' or 'patch'
to a file:
   If sh or bash:
     (command) 2>&1 | tee (output file)

For csh or tcsh:
   (command) |& tee (output file)

NOTE: grep root /etc/passwd
   look for sth like `/bin/csh`

183

If you get "make: *** No rule to make target `gconfig'. Stop

When you run make menuconfig
then do:

1) mkdir /usr/src/linux
2) move the source to /usr/src/
linux/
3) then unpack the source!
tar zxvf /path/to/linux-2.6.8.1.tar.gz

4) cd linux-2.6.8.1
& from here run
"make menuconfig"

973-251 9085

7 + код + номер + #

Related Titles from O'Reilly

Linux

Building Embedded Linux Systems

Building Secure Servers with Linux

The Complete FreeBSD, *4th Edition*

Even Grues Get Full

Exploring the JDS Linux Desktop

Extreme Programming Pocket Guide

GDB Pocket Reference

Knoppix Hacks

Knoppix Pocket Guide

Learning Red Hat Enterprise Linux and Fedora, *4th Edition*

Linux Annoyances for Geeks

Linux Cookbook

Linux Desktop Hacks

Linux Desktop Pocket Guide

Linux Device Drivers, *3rd Edition*

Linux in a Nutshell, *5th Edition*

Linux in a Windows World

Linux iptables Pocket Reference

Linux Multimedia Hacks

Linux Network Administrator's Guide, *3rd Edition*

Linux Pocket Guide

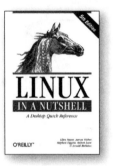

Linux Security Cookbook

Linux Server Hacks, *Volume 2*

Linux Unwired

Linux Web Server CD Bookshelf, *Version 2.0*

LPI Linux Certification in a Nutshell

Managing RAID on Linux

More Linux Server Hacks

OpenOffice.org Writer

Producing Open Source Software

Programming with Qt, *2nd Edition*

Root of all Evil

Running Linux, *5th Edition*

Samba Pocket Reference, *2nd Edition*

SUSE Linux

Test Driving Linux

Ubuntu Hacks

Understanding Linux Network Intervals

Understanding the Linux Kernel, *3rd Edition*

Understanding Open Source & Free Software Licensing

User Friendly

Using Samba, *2nd Edition*

Version Control with Subversion

skype → ykonoval58

O'REILLY®

Our books are available at most retail and online bookstores.

To order direct: 1-800-998-9938 • *order@oreilly.com* • *www.oreilly.com*

Online editions of most O'Reilly titles are available by subscription at *safari.oreilly.com*

The O'Reilly Advantage

Stay Current and Save Money

g1_strelkova@mail.ru
galinastrelkova1@yahoo.com